The Trouble with Higher Education

The Trouble with Higher Education is a powerful and topical critique of the Higher Education system in the UK, with relevance to countries with similar systems. Based on the authors' experiences that span over 30 years of fieldwork, the issues discussed focus on the problems facing the principal responsibilities of universities: teaching, learning and research.

The first half of the book identifies a number of problems that have followed the growth of mass education. It examines their causes and explains their damaging effects. The second half of the book offers a broad vision and makes a number of practical suggestions for ameliorating the problems and improving Higher Education. Supported by research, the suggestions include: ways of managing universities; proper inspection; better ways of organising students' learning; improving teaching and learning; better approaches to assessment; and the proper use of ideas such as learning outcomes.

Topics discussed include:

- Chronic under-funding, the replacement of student grants with loans and the introduction of tuition fees.
- The growth of managerialism.
- The emphasis on accountability and decline of trust.
- The growth of a competitive, market ethos.
- Modular degrees, knowledge treated as a commodity and students seen as customers.
- The drift towards a two-tiered system, with teaching colleges and research universities.
- Casualisation of the academic profession.

The Trouble with Higher Education is aimed primarily at a professional audience of academics, educationalists, managers, administrators and policy makers, but would interest anyone concerned about Higher Education. It is suited to professional development courses, and master's and doctoral level studies.

Trevor Hussey is Professor Emeritus of Philosophy at Buckinghamshire New University and is now a part-time tutor at the University of Oxford.

Patrick Smith is Professor of Learning and Teaching at Buckinghamshire New University.

The Trouble with Higher Education

A Critical Examination of our Universities

Trevor Hussey and Patrick Smith

Routledge
Taylor & Francis Group

NEW YORK AND LONDON

First published 2010
by Routledge
270 Madison Ave, New York, NY 10016

Simultaneously published in the UK
by Routledge
2 Park Square, Milton Park, Abingdon, Oxon OX14 4RN

Routledge is an imprint of the Taylor & Francis Group, an informa business

© 2010 Taylor & Francis

Typeset in Minion by RefineCatch Limited, Bungay, Suffolk
Printed and bound in the United States of America on acid-free paper by
Walsworth Publishing Company, Marceline, MO

Library of Congress Cataloging-in-Publication Data
Hussey, Trevor.
  The trouble with higher education : a critical examination of our
universities / Trevor Hussey and Patrick Smith.
    p. cm.
Includes bibliographical references and index.
  1. Education, Higher – Research.   2. Education, Higher – Aims and
objectives.   3. Universities and colleges – Research.   I. Smith, Patrick,
1931 Mar. 15–   II. Title.
LB2326.3.H87 2009
  378 – dc22

                                                    2009018687

ISBN10: 0–415–87197–2 (hbk)
ISBN10: 0–415–87198–0 (pbk)
ISBN10: 0–203–86634–7 (ebk)

ISBN13: 978–0–415–87197–6 (hbk)
ISBN13: 978–0–415–87198–3 (pbk)
ISBN13: 978–0–203–86634–4 (ebk)

Contents

Preface

This book has two main purposes. The first is to discuss some problems with higher education as it now exists in Britain. The second is to offer tentative solutions to some of these problems. Obviously, these purposes are based on the belief that our present higher education system has troubles worthy of discussion, hence those who believe it to be without blemish need read no further.

Our guess is that anyone who has even a slight acquaintance with higher education will still be reading. Whether you are a student, the parent of a student, an academic, a researcher in a university, an administrator or manager within education, an educationalist, a politician interested in education policy, an employer who uses the products of higher education, an educational journalist or indeed anyone who cares about our society and its future, you will be only too aware of the troubles of higher education. Of course, each will have a different list of troubles depending on their point of view and experience. This is inevitable with such a colossal and complicated phenomenon, and it makes it necessary for us to explain why we have chosen the topics discussed here and not others.

Both authors are practitioners who have spent almost four decades teaching in higher education, largely but not wholly, in Britain. We have experienced at first hand the massive increase in the number of students and institutions involved. We have witnessed at close quarters the growth of mass higher education and the transformation of what is offered in its name. As economists, managers and politicians will almost certainly point out, we are not economists, managers or politicians: we are academics. We are teachers and researchers who have laboured at the primary task of higher education: encouraging students to learn and to enjoy their learning. Consequently, we have focused in this book on those problems that have been most immediate and pressing in our efforts to teach and do research, but primarily to teach.

Before we mention the problems, we want to stress three things. First, we are wholly in favour of the expansion of higher education. The idea that only a tiny percentage of people, less than six per cent in the 1960s, are fit to receive a university education is both factually and morally wrong. Second, we are not criticising today's students or their efforts to obtain an education. As always, there are good, intelligent, industrious students and there are poor, demoralised and lazy students, and many in between. Those who struggle through the system and emerge with learning and the enthusiasm to use it, are to be congratulated. Our point is that in too many cases their struggle has been unnecessarily arduous: they have triumphed over difficulties that need not, and ought not, to have been put in their way. Third, we are not criticising all academics. Many have protested, or at least muttered, against the developments we have criticised here, and we hope that we are giving voice to their main concerns: indeed we thank those who have prompted our ideas and suggested our arguments. Some have shrugged at the seeming inevitability of the difficulties, and we hope that our positive ideas show that there are alternatives. Others have embraced with varying degrees of enthusiasm what we attack, and we will try to show that they were wrong.

The troubles we have picked out are those that most directly affect the students and teachers; many of which eventually impact upon those who employ the students. They are the problems that have arisen as a result of trying to offer mass education at as little cost as possible. These include the debased educational experience that many students now suffer; the struggle of academics to provide a good quality education to an immense herd of students; the distortion of learning under the pressure of trying to develop knowledge, understanding and enthusiasm as the herd gallops past, and the often doubtful quality of the result.

Alongside these troubles are the aggravating factors that have insinuated themselves as the higher education system has expanded so dramatically: the heavy, smothering overcoat of excessive and expensive management; the effects of a competitive, market place ethos, with its league tables and scramble for "customers"; the effects on students of the replacement of grants with loans and the pressure on them to fit learning in between shifts of work; the effects of chronic under-funding; the drift towards a two-tiered university system, and the insidious casualisation of the academic profession.

Our critics may see all this as just a rant against the inevitable difficulties of expanding the provision of higher education. If it is a rant, it is a rant with reason, in two senses. First, we have good reason to make the criticisms we do; for we believe that the blemishes we have identified are real and serious – they are damaging something of immense value. Second, we have tried to offer sound and cogent reasons why things have gone wrong, and we have even tried to suggest better alternatives.

Other critics may point to the problems we have overlooked or ignored. Here we can only repeat that we have chosen those that we have experienced most directly and which, we think, strike at the heart of what higher education is about. There are other serious problems which we have either omitted or merely gestured towards. For example, our whole education system can be accused of unfairness. The public schools educate a minute proportion of our children but dominate entry to our most prestigious universities. The latter plead that they have tried to remove barriers to state school pupils and that much of the connivance between the staff at public schools and their friends in the top universities has been eliminated, but the figures still show a shameful gap of opportunity. Unless state education is improved and university entry procedures are made entirely fair, or until critical attention is paid to our public school system, this will remain a serious fault with our system, but not one we will pursue here. It is primarily a problem with our unfair society, characterised as it is by social class divisions and a lack of social mobility.

We have restricted our attention largely to the bulk of the university system that has sprouted into being as the sector has expanded so dramatically since the 1960s. We are primarily concerned with that majority of universities and university colleges that compete for students in the new market place of higher education, after the élite institutions have creamed off their choice. None the less, we believe that both our critique and our positive suggestions have relevance for all those involved in higher education, in all institutions.

We have tried to produce a book that is accessible to lay readers as well as those engaged in education. We have kept the use of technical terms to a minimum and attempted to avoid, as much as possible, the thicket of acronyms surrounding the subject. However, it may be useful to explain a few of the central words here. The distinctions are current in Britain, although there is not unanimity about their meanings or their appropriateness. Our brief definitions are not intended as pieces of conceptual analysis, they merely indicate how we will employ the terms.

We shall take *tertiary* education to include any formal learning or training that follows after the normal school leaving age. Thus it succeeds primary and secondary education. It is the broadest term and includes both further and higher education. *Further* education is that form of tertiary education that is primarily or wholly focused on training for a practical craft, trade or vocation, and which does not involve a high proportion of theoretical content or emphasise critical analysis and evaluation. It is generally, although not necessarily, pursued for its extrinsic value; that is its usefulness in earning a living. In Britain further education is not normally taught in universities.

Higher education is that form of tertiary education undertaken in universities and some other specialist colleges. In Britain it is generally directed towards obtaining a first or bachelor degree, a master's degree or a doctorate. It is characterised by an emphasis upon the mastery of theories, technical and abstract concepts and general principles, together with skills of analysis and critical thinking. It is generally positioned within a distinct discipline, such as chemistry, history or English literature, or it may have a clear vocational purpose such as medicine or law, but it will always involve the investigation and mastery of broad, theoretical ideas and an emphasis on their critical evaluation. In further education success has been achieved when the student has mastered what the teacher has taught; in higher education success has been achieved when the student has subjected that teaching to severe questioning. Here we focus on higher education.

The term '*liberal education*' does not refer to another sub-division of tertiary education, but quite what it does refer to is a matter of debate (Fuller 1989; Ryan 1998; Axelrod 2002; Palfreyman 2008). We take liberal education to be an ideal: a form of, or approach to, higher education which is to be valued and sought after. It is higher education at its best. It is what we would wish for all university students. Seen in this way, liberal education attempts to develop certain values: a love of truth and critical enquiry; an appreciation of learning and scholarship; a commitment to accuracy, tolerance, fairness and honesty in intellectual matters; an acceptance of the value of judgements based on evidence and valid argument, and a passion for intellectual freedom. It sets out to engender skills and autonomy in learning, enquiry, imagination, questioning, argument, reasoning, and expression – both written and spoken – that have general application rather than being applied to a narrow, utilitarian end. A liberal education can be achieved in any discipline, whether the liberal arts or science, medicine, law or other ostensibly vocational courses, so long as the primary focus is on the critical evaluation of the content and not just the content itself.

We support the view that higher education should aspire to approximate as closely as possible to this ideal. Where it does so it will benefit the educated person throughout their life, and the society of which he or she is a member. A free and democratic society is predicated upon the ideal of a liberal education. It will equip the educated person to be of the greatest and most enduring value to the enterprises in which they are employed: the abilities and attitudes persisting long after time and change have rendered specific factual knowledge and narrow skills redundant. The idea of a liberal education embraces the now fashionable notions of transferable and generic skills but places them within a set of values that motivate their proper use. Being an old notion does not make it passé. We accept that this liberal ideal is difficult for both individuals and institutions to achieve but the degree to which they do is the mark of quality. There is room for applied and purely vocational training in which these liberal ideals hardly appear and it is of value to the student and the country, but it should not be passed off as higher education.

The book has a simple plan. The first seven chapters each discuss a different problem that troubles higher education as it is offered today. The remaining five chapters are more positive: they offer suggestions for better ways of proceeding. Chapter 9 requires special mention. It is much longer than the other chapters and consists of our broad view of the nature of a university and higher education, together with some of the options facing policy makers, ending with a statement of our general preferences concerning the future of higher education.

We would like to acknowledge with thanks the help and support given to us by our families, friends and colleagues.

1
The Troubles

The crowd has found the door into the secret garden. Now they will tear up the flowers by the roots . . . .

Alan Bennett (1969) *Forty Years On*: 78

There was a time, not so long ago, when the way into the secret garden of higher education was known to a very few. Over the last four decades in Britain, successive governments have striven to change things: from being the privilege of a middle class élite to being accessible to a huge section of society. In the 1960s only about one in 18 young people made their way to university; today it is over 40 per cent, and it is the declared aim of government that half of all young people will go through higher education.

In terms of national prudence and social justice, these changes are surely admirable. If Britain's economy is to prosper and its culture is to develop, we need to educate our people. We cannot compete in the global marketplace by our muscle power but must rely on knowledge, inventiveness and imagination. Success in science and technology will be vital in keeping the tills ringing; arts and sports make a huge contribution to the tourist industry, and all are of immense value to the quality of our lives. For the individual the advantages and benefits of an education are difficult to exaggerate: they are the means to a better quality, and even quantity, of life. It is surely right that the opportunity to benefit from higher education be not only increased but also spread to a wider social mix. People of both sexes in all social classes and of all ethnic origins must have a fair chance of a good education.

So, the expansion of higher education is laudable. But, agreement on this is the easy bit. The difficulties come when we ask exactly what is to constitute this expanded education and how it is to be paid for. Even here there are things that most commentators are likely to agree upon but, as soon as they are debated, doubts begin to appear about what has actually happened as higher education has been expanded and where we must go from here. Politicians, the general

1

public and those working in the area, including the students, are aware that all is not well. As we will show, the fruits are blemished and it is suspected that some at least are rotten.

Those responsible for the development of higher education over recent decades, and those who voted them into power, almost certainly wanted to preserve what was good about the existing system: they wanted to preserve its essential nature and quality. After all, it had served us rather well, at least since the reforms of the nineteenth century. One Cambridge college had produced almost as many Nobel Prize winners as the whole of France, so we must have been doing something right. The, perhaps naïve, vision was that the masses would share the same venerable system that the élite had enjoyed, albeit greatly expanded. Above all, the *quality* of the education would be maintained: there would be no dumbing down.

The new students would also experience much the same student life: perhaps lager would flow where once champagne was sipped, and not all the students would stroll in ancient stone quads, but there would be the red brick or even breeze-block equivalents. More importantly, students would receive the same level of intellectual stimulation, the same access to lively minds and vast stores of cultural excellence. There were to be many more students, but then there would be many more universities, staffed by many more academics. The gowns and gaudies might go but the students would still enjoy that ineffable experience of being marinaded in knowledge for three or four years while, at the same time, imbibing the rich culture that seasons the university diet. They would still be able to realise their potentials and pursue their personal ambitions, while acquiring a genuine education that would transform them as persons and enhance the rest of their lives.

Of course, changes would have to be made to cope with the increased numbers, but essentially the same old system could be stretched to suit, and the traditional academic calendar could be preserved. By modularisation and semesterisation we could achieve the flexibility and volume required, and these innovations would enable the whole business to be managed efficiently. If credit accumulation was introduced, students would be able to take up their studies, lapse and rejoin the system at a later date, or switch from one university to another carrying their credits with them. So, marriage, pregnancy or getting on a bike to find work would not prevent the masses from passing through the system.

Obviously this admirable expansion would have to be paid for, but the money would be found. Politicians on the right would see the economic benefits of the investment and those of the left would see the burgeoning social justice as more than worth the cost. Naturally, some changes would have to be made. The bright new institutions would have to be properly and professionally managed. If vast amounts of taxpayers' money were to be spent, governments could not pour them into the hands of be-tweeded dons. In the same way, the government might have to ensure the maintenance of academic standards. The seedling universities would not have the benefits of the sages lodged in the senior common rooms of Oxbridge colleges or the ancient system of Visitors to guide them and set the necessary standards. Independent bodies would be required for these purposes. Hence the creation of the Higher Education Quality Council and the Council for National Academic Awards (CNAA), and their successor the Quality Assurance Agency (QAA), and a number of other auditing bodies.

The 1980s brought a change of political climate and the vision was modified to embrace the invigorating cold shower of competition (Wright 2001). It was realised that another advantage of the great expansion was the creation of a market. The "customers", "consumers" or students would have a range of universities and colleges to choose from, and the "providers" would have to compete to attract them. This competition, it was argued, would ensure both quality and efficiency. Institutions that performed badly would have to reform themselves and those that were too profligate would suffer the consequences. League tables of performance data would be published to enable customers to make informed choices. Thus there would be a self-regulating mechanism to ensure that the vision was not only transformed into reality but that this was achieved in the most efficient way possible. The result would be more students having more choice but being educated at less expense to the taxpayer – the political equivalent of turning base metals into gold.

Unfortunately, this vision has not materialised in quite the sturdy forms and glowing colours that were so keenly anticipated. In quantitative terms there has been real progress. Many new universities have been founded and one time polytechnics and colleges of higher education have been transmogrified. Student numbers have risen in a very satisfying curve, and even if the social mix is not quite as egalitarian as would satisfy those committed to extending the franchise of education, students are now drawn from a much larger and more diverse population.

However, many critics remain. Those outside the "industry" of higher education – the politicians, employers, and media pundits – see waste and decadence. They point to "Mickey Mouse" degrees, the dumbing down of traditional degrees and trivial or ludicrous research. Universities are accused of doing anything to attract students and anything to grease their passage through the system and prevent them failing. Degrees are, it is said, given away, and an ever increasing proportion of students are awarded first class honours. There are stories of illiterate and incompetent graduates who have to be trained from scratch before they are capable of work. Others claim that the whole thing is too expensive and inefficient and that it is educating the wrong people in the wrong way and for the wrong jobs.

The academics inside the system complain of the bureaucracy and burden of management; the focus on monitoring and accountancy and the death of trust. They bemoan modularity and the commodification of knowledge; they wring their hands at the quality of their students, and resent those students acting like aggrieved customers when they don't receive the marks they expected. Above all they groan under the dispiriting and unrewarding burden of mass education: vast seas of anonymous faces that last only the first couple of weeks into the course, to be replaced by empty seats. Of course teaching can be a pleasing, rewarding and fulfilling experience and many academics chose their career for these reasons, but recent trends have made these benefits much more difficult to find, to the detriment of both teachers and taught. Those academics in the more prestigious universities can retreat into research but for the rest there is, too often, unremitting and thankless graft. Salaries are low by national and international standards, research money is difficult to find, the accustomed perks have been lost, and the traditional security replaced by casualisation and short term contracts.

The students have fared worst of all – although, because each intake has little idea of what went before, their afflictions are somewhat ameliorated: ignorance and innocence act as anaesthetics. None the less, the student experience has been transformed. The grant system has been replaced by work and debt. Students often work for more hours in a week than they attend college. Their studies are hard work but they are conducted on what energy and enthusiasm is left after stacking shelves or flipping burgers. In many of the new colleges they are encouraged by the system to see their education as a commodity to be bought at the lowest price. Each module has to be ticked off at the cost of an essay or an exam, and then off to the next. Too often the result is an "education" like a jigsaw puzzle composed of pieces selected randomly from different boxes.

One stark consequence of this transformation of the student's experience is that many drop out of the process. Whereas back in the 1960s a small proportion of students failed to complete their degrees now, after half a century of growth, one in ten fall out after the first year and well over 20 per cent fail to complete their degrees (Bourn 2007). Even an £800 million scheme to reduce university drop-out rates has failed to make any significant difference (Curtis 2008). It is often claimed that, by international standards, our drop-out rate is relatively low, but this is in part because our entry requirements are high: traditionally we have sowed sparsely and have not used university courses to thin out the crop, but this is changing now that so many more young people are being herded though the doors of universities. Those that survive the course may find that their employment prospects and earning power are not so very different from their friends who left schooling at 16.

Measured in financial terms, there have been some efficiencies of scale. To produce each graduate it now costs much less than that paid for the 1960s product, but this ignores the reduction in the quality of provision and the cost of those who drop out. The cost in human terms of failing to complete cannot be quantified in cash but it is deplorable. The trampled hopes and ambitions, the evaporated enthusiasm, the humiliation and sense of defeat, not to mention the wasted time, all taint people for life. Academics also feel the loss and let-down of depleted numbers. Those in the system have made changes in an attempt to increase retention of students. Course structures and teaching methods have been modified, induction courses elaborated, student support services have proliferated, "buddying" and mentoring programmes have been tried, all with varying results; however the haemorrhage continues.

There have been numerous responses from governments to try to overcome some of the problems mentioned above: changes in funding, league tables of institutions, modification of the way the monitoring is done by QAA, changes in the student grant and loan provision, bursaries and so forth, but the problems merely persist or mutate into new problems. One change that has insinuated itself, provoked at least in part by the spectre of international competition, is the separation of higher education institutions into two kinds: those that teach and those that do research. This, it is thought, will enable the leading universities to keep pace with the great universities of America and elsewhere, while retaining the means of mass producing graduates. It will preserve for the élite their Elysium and give to the rest what the nation deems necessary.

It will be interesting to see the effect on the careers and salaries of students passing through the two systems. Already there is a very significant difference between the experience of those students who attend the older universities and those who pass through the newer institutions; a difference emphasised by their contrasting drop-out rates. We can only speculate about the effect that it will have on academics but, given the need to build a CV full of publications, it may be yet another blunder. Of course teaching is a vitally important part of higher education, but most academics, even those who see their main priority and chief talent as teaching, will hesitate before allowing themselves to be caught in a teaching ghetto.

We can be justifiably proud of our higher education system, but our capacity to mutilate it must also be recognised. Our most prestigious universities appear in the top ten in world rankings (Times Higher Education 2007) but a huge proportion of our students attend very different institutions and they are our primary concern here. This is not the place for a detailed discussion of the history of higher education but it is important and sobering to note that the path from the mediaeval *studium generale* in Oxford to the present plethora of institutions has been bedevilled by errors and misjudgements of policy: there are plenty of precedents for today's predicament. Rulers, governments, the church, the aristocracy, the gentry, industry and the university authorities themselves have repeatedly manoeuvred and manipulated the system to gain their own ends or protect their own interests, often with disastrous consequences.

For example, after the Reformation, Oxford and Cambridge became the domain of the Anglican Church and they set about excluding first the Catholics and later the Dissenters – that is to say, those lecturers and fellows who refused to accept the Book of Common Prayer and ordination into the Church of England. The consequences were serious: apart from the social injustice involved, it caused an appalling loss of talent and intellect. It hampered the establishment of the experimental sciences in the universities, especially in Oxford, and neither institution played any significant part in the industrial revolution that transformed our society (Darlington 1970). The rule that not even professors of natural science could be appointed without swearing to uphold the Thirty-Nine Articles was not removed until 1871. The treatment of women is another example of the establishment's resistance to change. It was not until the mid-nineteenth century that women's colleges appeared, and women were not permitted to take degrees in Oxford until 1920, while Cambridge held out until 1948, and even then restricted the number to six hundred. Today, women outnumber men in the United Kingdom's universities.

Of course, these historical examples, and the many more that could be added, do not establish that today's policy makers are wrong-headed, self-serving or malevolent, but they do underline the need to examine critically what is happening in our own time. Indeed, the Dearing Report (1997) showed that the capacity to get things wrong was still with us at the end of the twentieth century. It identified several recent government errors and mis-calculations: amongst others, those concerning inadequate funding and staffing for the massive increase in student numbers. The report said that 'The expansion was . . . much faster than the Government had initially envisaged and there was insufficient thought about the potential effects of a progressively reducing unit of funding' (Dearing 1997: 3.115). The report also pointed out that the difference in funding levels between the older and the newer universities was an historical anomaly with little or no rational justification.

Dearing's strictures had little or no effect. A recent report has shown that the pressure continues unabated to process more and more students "efficiently"; that is to say with no commensurate increase in staff and resources (Tysome 2006). The Higher Education Statistics Agency showed that the student-to-staff ratios (SSRs) in higher education increased between 2000–01 and 2003–04, from just over 16:1 to more than 18:1; which is higher than in state secondary schools. Some institutions had SSRs of over 30:1 and the highest was 46:1. It is evident that it remains important to question what has been done to, and by, the institutions of higher education over the last few decades. Clearly the policies pursued by both politicians and educators have not had entirely benign results: there are serious problems with the present system.

So, the expansion of higher education achieved over the last half century, although estimable in principle, is in practice beset by disfigurements and serious problems. It is subject to criticisms from those who pay for it, those who work in it, those who are processed though it, and those who use its products.

Good intentions have not succeeded in producing what was envisioned and the chief faults lie with the system we have produced, not with the youngsters who suffer it. In his play *Forty Years On*, first performed in 1968, Alan Bennett has the public school headmaster say, with melancholic resignation:

> The crowd has found the door into the secret garden. Now they will tear up the flowers by the roots, strip the borders and strew them with paper and broken bottles.
>
> (1969: 78)

But the headmaster was wrong. The crowd has been *led* to the door and *ushered* into the garden by its proprietors, and it is the proprietors who are largely to blame for the desecration.

Let us be clear. We welcome the crowd into higher education but believe that this can be done without covering the garden with tarmac. We believe that the 1960s vision was wholly laudable and that it is possible for a wealthy nation to realise it in a much better form than achieved so far. We must try to preserve the essential nature and quality of what we had, and offer an educational experience that is enriching and life enhancing. Students must receive a real education that satisfies them, those who teach them, and those who subsequently employ them. Our aim should be a 'liberal education'. We must reduce the waste and hurt involved in the dropping out of students, and all this must be achieved within a system that can handle huge numbers of disparate students from a wide variety of backgrounds. What is more the system must remain efficient and cost effective. Impossible? Perhaps, but given the present state of affairs it is at least worth trying to debate the problems and tender some suggestions towards improvement.

As we have indicated, the problems that beset higher education in Britain, and their causes, are diverse, ranging from the political, ideological and economic to the design and delivery of particular teaching sessions or the provision of student accommodation. Clearly it is not possible to attempt a discussion of them all. Since the authors are neither politicians nor economists this book will focus primarily on issues that arise within the "industry" itself, with only the occasional venture into the wider terrain. However, much of what is discussed here about Britain's universities will be of relevance to many other countries with similar systems and troubles.

In Chapters 2 to 7 we will take up what we see as the most serious problems and defects in the practices of higher education and try to expose and examine their origins and causes. From there on the book will take on a more positive task, outlining a constructive view of a university and offering suggestions for reform. These suggestions will be radical but we hope to show that they are both necessary and practical.

2
Expansion and Distortion

In this chapter we will begin our examination of the expansion of higher education and look at the nature and effects of this transformation. We will discuss the principal structural changes: the growth in size of the sector, the greatly increased diversity of the students entering into it, and the reduction in funding for each student. We will see that some of the intended effects were not realised as envisaged, and they were accompanied by unintended effects of great significance. The education system has certainly grown, but it is not just a bigger version of the original or an unqualified improvement: the growth has involved twists and distortions.

The recent rapid expansion of higher education is the latest phase of a very long historical process, but it is unique in its magnitude. With a few hesitations and reverses, university education in Britain has been expanding ever since the first mention of Oxford as a centre of learning in the late eleventh century. During the last third of the twelfth century, Oxford was being referred to as a *studium generale*, indicating that students were gathering there from a wide area. At first the expansion was modest: Oxford was joined by Cambridge and henceforth these institutions grew by accreting colleges. Their monopoly was broken in the fifteenth century when three universities, St. Andrews, Glasgow and Aberdeen, were established in Scotland. In the aftermath of the Reformation several new colleges were founded in Oxford and Cambridge, and in the sixteenth century colleges were established in Edinburgh and Dublin. The nineteenth century saw a much more rapid increase as more than a dozen new universities and colleges were started in London and several other major cities in England, Wales and Ireland. Another five universities were founded in the first decade of the twentieth century and by 1938, just prior to the Second World War, there were about 46,000 students in higher education in the United Kingdom; about a quarter of whom were women.

After the war the growth accelerated again as successive governments, with their eyes on our international competitors, stressed the need for a better educated workforce. By 1960 the number of students in higher education in the UK had reached almost 200,000 (Dearing 1997: 3.4). However, following the Robbins Committee Report in 1963 the numbers increased with unprecedented rapidity for the rest of that decade; then rose more slowly through the 1970s and early 1980s, accelerating again in the late 1980s and 1990s. The 1992 Further and Higher Education Act saw a big expansion of the university system with many polytechnics and other colleges gaining that title. However, during the mid and late 1990s governments dithered about the need for, and cost of, continued expansion. The situation of the universities became desperate, principally because their funding, both for teaching and research, had been greatly reduced. Higher education was in a shambles.

Ron Dearing, now a Lord, was asked to prepare a report on higher education and, after a hectic series of meetings and gathering of submissions from interested parties, his committee produced their report in 1997. It was a huge tome which concluded with 93 recommendations, and it has had an effect upon higher education in the UK almost commensurate with its size. The recommendations were generally very positive: the expansion should continue; money should be invested in research to maintain the high status of our universities; teaching in higher education should be more professional; maintenance grants should be continued, and so on. However, the report also made a more debatable recommendation. It suggested that students should pay tuition fees of £1,000 per year of study. This would be paid after graduation and there should be means-tested grants available for less-well-off students.

By the time of the Dearing Report in 1997 there were more than 1.6 million students in higher education, of which well over a million were studying full-time or sandwich courses (Dearing 1997: 3.5); there are around 2 million today. Put another way, in the early 1960s only about 5.5 per cent of our young people were in full-time higher education, but by 1997 this had risen to nearly 33 per cent overall, and around 45 per cent in Scotland and Northern Ireland. Today the average for the UK is over 42 per cent and there is a government target of 50 per cent by 2010. Since Dearing, numbers have continued to increase modestly with only minor reverses, such as the fall in applications when universities began charging top-up fees in 2006.

As well as these increases in numbers, this period also saw important changes in the composition of the student population. The proportion of women students increased dramatically: from 37 per cent of the total in 1979–80 to 51 per cent in 1996–97, since when it has continued to rise at a slower rate until today it is just over 54 per cent. There were also changes in the representation of students from the various socio-economic groups. All groups shared in the increase in youngsters going into higher education, but the Group I (Professional) took the greatest advantage. Between 1991–92 and 1995–96 the number of young people from Group I increased from 55 per cent to 80 per cent, while Group V (Unskilled) increased from the lamentably low level of about 5 per cent to the marginally better 10 per cent (Dearing 1997: 3.14).

These class differences are striking and lamentable, but obviously it is not simply a matter of an unfair university system. The principal problem lies with the schools. Class and racial inequalities stain our pre-school, primary and secondary education systems, so that the pattern is deeply engraved before the tertiary stage is reached. The picture is exacerbated by the dominance of the public schools, which function so as to magnify the inequalities. None the less, there is ample room for improvement in the university sector where the situation described by Dearing has not improved significantly in the years since his report and, as the tussle to raise fees continues, it is likely to worsen (Davies, Slack, Hughes, Mangan and Vigurs 2008).

There have also been very significant changes in the ethnic mix in the student population since the 1960s and Dearing (1997: 3.13) points out that 'In aggregate, students from ethnic minorities are more than proportionately represented in higher education'. The report also noted that a greater proportion of these were mature students and that they were concentrated in the newer, post 1992, universities. Black and ethnic minority students now comprise about 22 per cent of entrants into English universities (Bourn 2007). However, in 2006 it was pointed out that the, then 19, Russell Group universities put together had fewer black (Afro-Caribbean) students than London's Metropolitan University (Curtis 2006).

Today, England alone has around 78 universities, 14 general colleges, which include university colleges, and 40 specialist institutions, with over 1.7 million full- and part-time students in higher education. The UK has around 120 universities, 20 of which constitute the élite Russell Group, which includes Oxford and Cambridge. So, from a time in the 1960s when only one in 18 young people went to university – and the vast majority of them from middle-class, professional families – we are now approaching a time when one in two will do so, and from an enormously more varied population.

We wish to stress two points. First, political expediency is seen most starkly concerning the financing of higher education. Making speeches about the need for more graduates brings earnest applause, but raising taxes to pay for them brings only trouble. Of course, public spending on higher education has increased in real terms during recent decades, from £4.7 billion in 1997–98 to £9.5 billion in 2007–08, a cash increase of 102 per cent and 59 per cent in real terms (UCU 2006: Section 7). However, this is a misleading picture. As the Dearing Report (Dearing 1997: 3.95) pointed out, between 1976 and 1995 the amount paid to universities and colleges for each student had fallen in real terms by more than 40 per cent because of the rapid increase in numbers. More recent government statistics showed that funding per student fell by 36 per cent between 1989 and 1997, but these figures were accompanied by a claim that the government is reversing years of under-investment (DfES 2003). Unfortunately the facts suggest that this is a very modest reversal even by the DfES's own figures. At 2001–02 prices, funding in 1989–90 was just under £8,000 per student; it fell to a fraction over £5,000 by 1997–98 and remained just below £5,000 until 2005–06, if the student fees contribution is deducted. If the student fees contribution is included the figure rises to around £5,400 in 2005–06. Thus it remains the case that today's universities are educating a greatly increased number of students at a greatly reduced funding per student. This is despite the fact that the '. . . Exchequer receives associated tax from higher salaries of graduates amounting to 11 per cent over and above the cost of higher education' (Bourn 2007: 6). [The Department for Education and Skills (DfES) was replaced in June 2007 by the Department for Children, Schools and Families (DCSF) and the Department for Innovation, Universities and Skills (DIUS).]

Governments have adopted various manoeuvres aimed at restraining expenditure while continuing to expand higher education. The most important and far reaching of these was the ending of student grants in 1998. The government took up the Dearing recommendations rather selectively. They decided to introduce tuition fees but made them £3,000 and payable upfront, and they omitted to provide grants for the poorer students. They also ended maintenance grants. This meanness got them into trouble.

Public protests and revolts within the ranks of MPs in 2004 eventually persuaded the government to change its mind. From September 2006 universities were allowed to charge tuition fees of up to £3,000 per year (£3,225 in 2009) to be repayable after graduation and only if the graduate had a certain level of income. The majority have decided to charge the full amount for most courses, accompanied by a plea that they be allowed to increase them in future. Means-tested grants were re-introduced to help less-well-off families and maintenance loans were offered which could also be paid back after graduation. The universities have introduced various bursaries and discounts to try to attract students. Devolution of political control in the UK has complicated matters: Scottish students studying in Scottish universities pay no tuition fees but must make a single means-tested payment of over £2,000 after graduating, and even this is in the process of being dropped; while there are special maintenance grants in Wales and Northern Ireland to benefit their indigenous students.

The heads of the leading universities have discussed a rise of top-up fees to around £6,000 and even £10,000 for some science degrees (Meikle and Lewis 2007). As several leading universities have accumulated large deficits they are scratching at the door of government, knowing that there is to be a review in 2009. The overall result of all this is that students pay for their education while, in effect, we now have a system of income-contingent grants and loans which, it is claimed, will favour students from lower-income families.

Whether this will help to remove the shameful class differences in access to higher education remains to be seen, but the evidence seems to be pointing in the opposite direction. While the number of applications for entry to university continues to rise, those from poorer families are levelling off. Research produced by Staffordshire University has found that financial considerations, especially fear of debt, are major factors in deterring students from poorer families from applying for university, and youngsters from these families are more likely to choose a local institution so as to reduce costs, while middle-class students tend to apply to what they consider the best university, wherever it may be located. The existence of bursaries is not as helpful as it might be because students rarely consider them before applying and, even then, the bursary has to be large to make a significant difference (Davies, Slack, Hughes, Mangan and Vigurs 2008).

The outlook is not bright: as Stephen Ball (2008) argues, recent changes in our children's education system by a Labour government – a *Labour* government – have moved it back towards the class divisions of Victorian times. The upper class has its public schools, subsidised by their charity status; the middle class has its faith schools, and the working class has what is left. There is a danger that this pattern is being duplicated in the university sector with the Russell Group, the red-brick universities and the teaching factories. The evidence collected by Wilkinson and Pickett (2009) shows the stark consequences of income inequality for educational performance, drop-out rates and literacy levels, alongside a wide range of other effects. Yet we appear to be building inequality into the very structure of our society. The machinery of segregation may move slowly but it moves none the less.

These recent changes have transformed the experience of higher education for all but the wealthiest of students and, as we will see, it has had a major impact upon life within colleges. The justification for ending the traditional grant system and making students purchase their education generally includes the claim that graduates enjoy a much higher level of earnings throughout their working lives. However, while that may have been true when only a small élite passed through higher education, it will ring increasingly hollow as the proportion of graduates approaches one in two.

In brief, the number of students in higher education has been increased very rapidly while the funding, both that paid to the institutions and that paid to the students, has been reduced or transformed into loans. Students now buy their education.

The second point we want to stress is that, as student numbers have been increased, this has inevitably drawn in a much more *diverse* population. Today's students come from much more varied cultural and ethnic backgrounds, and they have had very different educations from those of the middle-class and upper-class élites that dominated the university intake of 50 years ago. Their aspirations and interests, as well as their abilities and knowledge are different. So too are the attitudes and values of their families and the communities from which they come. We now select from a population of young people, most of whom do not belong to a sub-culture that expects to do well at school and who take university education for granted. The increases in the number of women and of mature students have brought with them increased strains on the traditional system, especially concerning family commitments, child care and so forth. This suggests what experience confirms – that the needs of today's student population are very different from those of the past.

Unfortunately, institutional inertia caused, at least in part, by lack of money together with political expediency, have ensured that today's students pass through a similar kind of institution to those of the 1950s, but with less resources to spend. There have been changes but not enough and not always of the right kind. Dearing (1997: 3.56–3.60) found that both teaching staff and students complained about the effects of mass education: the lack of academic support; the inadequate feedback on students' work; the inadequate library resources and so on – complaints that are still heard today. It is not surprising that there is discontent and that large numbers of students are dropping out.

One thing that has not changed significantly is the academic calendar. We have retained the basic three terms per year. It has been imposed on the new population of students with only trivial changes, presumably because it is seen as self-evidently right – an arrangement sanctified by the wisdom of the ages. The traditional three terms still follow the historical demands of the ecclesiastical and agrarian culture in which they originated. The first term starts at the end of harvest and lasts until Christmas; the second stretches from Christmas till Easter, and the third runs from Easter to haymaking. Some universities, not Oxbridge of course, have adopted the semester system popular in America, whereby the year is divided into three semesters of equal length. Unfortunately, in our adaptation of this idea the two teaching semesters usually sit uncomfortably on top of the three terms: Christmas comes too soon and Easter keeps wandering about according to an arcane formula based on the phases of the moon.

Similarly, the length of undergraduate degrees has been retained as the system has been expanded. In England and Wales most degree programmes are three years long, with a few special degrees running for four years. In Scotland degree courses are often of four years' duration. This system is maintained not only by the institutions but also by whatever grant or loan arrangements the country provides, which makes it difficult to take longer in gaining a degree. Within such timetables, the fate of students is usually assessed at the end of each year and, if they are found satisfactory, they move up to the next level of difficulty. Consequently, the typical pattern, in England and Wales at least, is that students enter a rigid calendar in which they must move on at 12-monthly intervals and complete their studies in three years, whatever their individual needs or capabilities. There are generally provisions for re-taking all or part of the work of a year or semester, but there are severe consequences for the individuals who have to avail themselves of them and for the universities that allow them to do so. In Chapter 11 we will question the wisdom of these traditional practices and suggest alternatives.

The consequences for the student who fails a semester or year include not only the loss of time and separation from friends in the original cohort, but also financial penalties. The Higher Education Funding Council (Hefce) pays universities for teaching students but withholds funds if students do not progress or complete. Attempts to accommodate the changed nature of the student intake have included various induction programmes and foundation years, but the constraints of both the traditional calendar and finances militate against radical changes. To make the first year too gentle is to make the second and third years more demanding. A consequence of this failure to respond to the changed needs of the student population is a serious rate of dropping out, especially during the first year of the degree.

One response is to argue that the new student population contains a much higher proportion of people with limited abilities, low motivation, low aspirations, little family support and no proper understanding of what to expect at university. Consequently, we must *expect* a larger drop-out rate than we saw when a well off élite regularly took up what they considered their birthright. However, this response is, at best, a mere description of the problem and, at worst, a case of blaming the victims. If the nation needs more graduates then it has to widen the range of people from whom it recruits its students, and if these students have different needs from those recruited in the past, these needs must be met. Failure to do so is distressing to the students, frustrating to their teachers and profoundly uneconomical for the country. We shall argue that the system of higher education needs to be changed in more radical ways if these problems are to be solved.

Alongside these changes there have been others. University research is under pressure. In press articles and letters many academics have expressed anxiety at the closing of science departments, especially concerning physics and chemistry (for examples see Guardian 2006; Taylor 2006; and Kroto 2007). Government support for research has been increased in recent years but accompanied by various schemes to keep down costs to the taxpayer. As mentioned earlier, there has been a trend towards concentrating research funding in a small number of "élite" institutions. The chief motive is to ensure that we keep pace with – or don't trail too far behind – the great American universities and those burgeoning in China, India and Japan. Another aim is to ensure that the research money is well spent – that is given to the most able and effective researchers. These are important aims but they have to be balanced against the potentially harmful effects of a two-tier university system.

Universities have also been encouraged to turn to industry for research money and to try to do more "applied" research which has a saleable outcome.

Again, there is obvious sense in this but also dangers. If universities are to fulfil their traditional roles of social critics they need to be independent of both governments and commerce. Similarly, if science is to prosper it must include pure science: research which is done in pursuit of knowledge for its own sake and without any obvious prospect of profits. Traditionally this has been the role of the universities. There may never be a commercial reward from pure science and it is unwise to expect it, but there are many examples of great benefits in the long run. In the case of applied research, there must be freedom to publish results whatever they are – even if they harm or undermine a commercial product. The commercial world also provides examples of activities that universities ought to shun. For example, some aspects of arms manufacturing, the tobacco industry, and the way the pharmaceutical industry focuses on profitable areas and neglects diseases and communities that are unprofitable.

Similar points can be made concerning the humanities and arts. The study of philosophy, history, literature, theatre, dance, sport, the arts, crafts and so on is essential for our cultural life and commercial well-being. Our ability to create and question philosophical, theological, political, social and moral developments is crucial to our society and its future. These studies must not be neglected or offered only to those from certain social backgrounds: they should be prominent in as many universities as possible. The trend in many of the newer universities to offer applied, job-oriented courses may be laudable, but again there are dangers. A course on how to manage music or dance events may be useful but it will not produce the music and dance to be managed, nor is it likely to produce a critical, questioning attitude towards what is on offer.

This last point touches on a very old and very troublesome feature of our culture. In Britain there has long been a serious rift between those subjects seen as academically respectable and worthy of a university education, and those deemed mere crafts and worthy of being learned on the job or, at most, on a day-release course. The first are the domain of the educated gentleman, the second the burden of the labouring classes. This cultural prejudice has blighted our society for centuries, despite the arguments of such as Ruskin, William Morris, the Arts and Crafts Movement and numerous socialist and liberal thinkers.

The great expansion in higher education and the widening chasm between the top institutions and those at the bottom has seen some muddying of this cultural stream. To the accompaniment of sneers and head shaking, many universities have begun to offer applied, job-oriented degrees, in such subjects as sports management, TV production, media studies, leisure and tourism and so on. In an economy dominated by service industries, where the manufacturing sector is shrinking and insurance policies or bank loans count as "products", this may be an inevitable and even desirable development. (While management, accountancy, medicine and law are also applied and job-oriented degrees they are, of course, respectable.) However, if such courses come to dominate the programmes of the "lesser" teaching universities while being eschewed by the "superior" research institutions, this will help to perpetuate and exacerbate the damaging prejudice. The current pattern of expansion appears to be heading inexorably in that direction.

In this chapter we have outlined the political, economic, structural and demographic factors that have influenced the recent massive expansion in higher education in the United Kingdom, and we have argued that, while the expansion is real enough, it has been carried out in a way that has caused several distortions and disfigurements. We have failed to respond to the different needs of the new breed of students, drawn from a very different social and cultural background from that of the students of the mid-twentieth century. We have also begun to do serious long-term damage to what is valuable about a university system. It is as if we are unable or unwilling to offer the masses what we offer the élites. However, there are other features of our new system of higher education that are more subtle but equally pernicious. These are the subject of the following chapters.

3
A Mycelium of Managers

I cannot by any means approve of those meddlesome and restless char-
acters who, called neither by birth nor fortune to the management of
public affairs, are yet forever thinking up some new reform.
Descartes (1985: 1637) *The Philosophical Writings of Descartes*: 118

The present problems with higher education are not just the result of increased
student numbers, reduced funding and a greater diversity of students. The
difficulties have been exacerbated by the convergence of two other major
factors. One is the marked rise of *managerialism* within education and the
other is the advance of a *market and consumerist ethos*. These developments
are large topics which will occupy much of the first half of the book. They may
sound rather abstract and harmless, even benign, but there are good arguments, backed up by substantial evidence, to demonstrate that they are doing
serious damage within education – not to mention other areas of society.
These two factors work together and feed on each other in ways that have
transformed higher education for both staff and students. Like grey squirrels,
they were introduced for good reasons but have had unforeseen and damaging
consequences.

The first of these insidious factors is the growth of managerialism and the
ethos of accountability within higher education. It is not a controversial or
unreasonable idea that an institution or organisation will function better if it
is managed – that is organised and regulated. Those who are engaged in the
primary activities of the institution – that is to say, those who are doing
the work for which the institution exists and is funded – may need assistance
and facilitation. They may find the tasks of management an encumbrance or
burden and so require help in carrying them out. Academics, for example, are
experts in their disciplines, not in management. There may well be aspects of
the work, such as financial and legal matters, where experts are a necessity. For
such reasons managerial assistance is an inevitable and beneficial part of any

institution. However, managerialism is quite another matter. Of course educational institutions must be run properly, and this will require managers, but there are dangers in what is done and how it is done. Several educationalists have argued, or railed, against the growth of managerialism (e.g. Power 1997; Shore and Selwyn 1998; Cunningham 2000; Strathern 2000; Wright 2001; Loughlin 2002; Evans 2004; Docherty 2008; Kealey 2008).

Nigel Wright (2001: 281) argues that 'Crucially managerialism needs to be apprehended first as a set of beliefs, an ideology, and second as giving rise to a set of practices.' He follows Hartley (1983) in seeing an ideology as a structure or framework of ideas, beliefs and values which is essentially political in nature – in the sense that it concerns arranging and distributing the resources within a section of society. Such an ideology is developed and maintained by a social group which holds that it justifies what the group believes it ought to do.

This thesis can be interpreted in several ways, but we suggest that chief amongst the beliefs implicit in managerialism is the idea that management in itself is of greater importance than the primary activities that are being managed. The efficiency, discipline and organisation imposed by managers are the prime vehicles for success, whatever the enterprise. The slogan 'managers must have the right to manage' must be interpreted in the strong sense that the workforce are accountable to managers, not the other way round; and not interpreted merely in the weak sense that managers should be allowed to practise their expertise. The ideology teaches that the successes of an institution are due to its management and its failures to obdurate and unco-operative workers. Thus any problems must be overcome by strengthening and extending the managerial system; by modifying the primary activities to make them more manageable, which will include making them easier to audit and monitor, and by making the workforce more accountable for what they do – that is to say by strengthening the organisation's managerial hierarchy.

As more public money, however inadequate, has been spent on the system, so governments have lost their faith in academic institutions to spend it efficiently. Universities have been "encouraged" to adopt ever more elaborate accounting and managerial systems. The 1992 Further and Higher Education Act imposed two bodies designed to audit the institutions and assess the quality of their performance: the Higher Education Quality Council and the Funding Councils. These have transmuted into the Quality Assurance Agency (QAA) in 1997 to cover England, Wales and Northern Ireland and the Higher Education Funding Council (Hefce). Scotland has its own Scottish Qualifications Authority (SQA) and there are several professional bodies that audit and accredit the quality of awards in their fields. Understandably, Hefce keeps track of the progress of each individual student before parting with funds for their education.

Alongside this, the Research Assessment Exercise (RAE) regularly assesses each institution to judge whether it deserves research funding and, if so, how much. Add to this the demands of other funding agencies; the constant task of raising funds; the need to prepare and polish statistics for league tables; the competition for students with other colleges, hiring and firing staff, complying with health and safety and employment legislation, the need to manage land, buildings and other assets, negotiate with trades unions and so forth, and it is not difficult to understand why universities have acted as hosts to the growth of formidable bureaucracies.

These changes are, in great part, a response to the pressures applied by external bodies, especially the QAA. The QAA is a powerful body which audits universities and colleges, usually one department or faculty at a time. Their visits to colleges have been times of intense stress and frenetic activity in the past, and even now that a "softer approach" has been adopted, they remain events of enormous importance. The grade they give to an institution becomes a public indicator of its quality. No college can afford to do badly in the eyes of the QAA if it wants to keep its reputation in the marketplace.

One way of expressing the problem of managerialism, as described above, is as follows. Universities and colleges exist to provide education and undertake research: their primary purpose is to fulfil these social needs, and it is for these functions that the taxpayers and students find the money. The people who carry out the primary tasks of educating and researching are the academics. Managerial systems are brought into being to serve – to facilitate and assist – the academic staff. However, once these managerial bureaucracies are brought into being their first tendency is to proliferate; their second tendency is to become focused upon their own concerns rather than the concerns of those they were created to serve, and their third tendency is to change what they manage for their own purposes and to the detriment of the original function.

The similarity to a fungal attack is striking. Gradually, classrooms are converted into offices, academics become a decreasing proportion of the workforce and an increasing proportion of the available funds is spent on the non-academic sector. Soon it is the managers who hold the purse strings and have the power. The primary activities for which the institutions exist to perform become an inconvenient source of problems, and it is at this point that the managerial bureaucracy begins to modify what it manages. Each change is designed to make the manager's task easier. To manage requires information about what is being managed; this requires systems of audit – a means of measurement. Slowly, and sometimes not so slowly, the primary functions of the institutions are modified until they suit the functions of management rather than those for whom they were intended. What is taught and how it is taught and assessed changes to facilitate not education but audit or the latest fashion "encouraged" by the QAA.

Even the vocabulary begins to transmute as managerial discourse becomes the norm. We talk of "mission statements", "strategic plans", "performance indicators", "audit trails", "accountability", "quality assurance", "criteria" of this and that. Line managers appear where once there were senior colleagues and deans are subtly transmuted into executive deans. As language changes, so does thinking, and as thinking changes so does action and with it the whole experience of education. One consequence for the academic enclave has been a huge increase in form filling, paper shuffling and other administrative work which has had a mainly detrimental effect upon teaching and research, not to mention the morale of those involved (Evans 2004; Kord and Wilson 2006). Another consequence has been the growth of a vast committee structure organised in chains, up which minutes are passed and down which pass instructions from the burgeoning directorate.

Yet another consequence has been the steady loss of status, power, working conditions and remuneration relative to the administration hierarchy. This process is illustrated graphically by an anonymous letter to the *Guardian* (July 10th 2007) reporting that one (named) university:

> has seen the proliferation of managers, business development units, press and publicity officers etc, yet when teaching staff leave, there is a battle to get them replaced. Instead, departments are encouraged to rely on sessional staff, whose contracts have been reduced from 15 weeks to 12 weeks, meaning they mark work in their own time. Student numbers are being doubled and staff told to "address their delivery" (ie "teach less").
>
> During the current vice chancellor's reign he has changed the management structure of the university. Each school had a director (now on £70,000), but they now have to report to the six deans of faculty (whose recent self-awarded pay rise takes them to £97,000) who in turn report to the five pro vice chancellors (£150,000). That's an additional £1,332,000 – and that does not include the cost of all these new managers' offices or support staff.
>
> Perhaps the universities should have to reveal exactly how many of their staff come into direct contact with students. That would be some indication of if they are spending money wisely.

One of the central assumptions underlying this mycelium-like growth of managerial structures is that the quality of the "product", and the satisfaction of the "customer", can only be assured if those at the chalk face can *demonstrate* that quality is being delivered. It follows that academic staff must meet certain criteria and show that various performance indicators have been reached. In this way their "output" can be monitored and audited. As Michael Loughlin (2002) has argued, this presupposes that the managers have identified and described what constitutes quality and that it can be objectively measured. It also assumes that if managers receive the right signals at their end of the audit trail then quality has been assured. Of course, managerial satisfaction is just as likely to be achieved when the teaching staff are so busy ensuring that the right signals are sent that they are distracted from their proper duties. Loughlin argues that 'the purpose of all this quality jargon is not to improve services, but rather to locate power in the hands of those who control the "quality mechanisms" and to "deliver support" for government policies' (p. 20). This may seem cynical, but not when set in the context of an education system that has seen real quality evaporate in the sunshine of the new regime.

A stark example of these developments is the bureaucratic structures required to get a college through a QAA visitation. This has to be experienced to be believed. Hierarchies of committees have to be established and connected by elaborate paper trails; each module must be swaddled in documents; academic audit trails must be constructed; student complaint and counselling systems documented; learning outcomes enumerated; assessment criteria issued, and so on. The result is the construction of a vast paper soufflé at which the visitors may salivate, but which sags out of sight immediately the QAA visit is over. The contrast with the visit of profoundly useful, if underpaid, external examiners is most striking.

The power of such bodies as the QAA to force universities to change internally and set up permanent and complex managerial systems has been the subject of serious criticism (Power 1997; Strathern 2000). Thomas Docherty, a Professor of English and of comparative literature at the University of Warwick, has raised concern about the pressure from the QAA intended to turn universities into instruments for vocational training, producing people with 'transferable skills'. He has expressed his feelings about the organisation with only modest constraint:

> At the centre of this instrumentalisation of English and of the University has been a massive culture of mistrust, essentially put in place by the conservatives (sic) who systematically attacked the public sector – and the public sphere – in the 1980s and since. We must all surely agree that the establishment of the Quality Assurance Agency was the worst thing to happen to higher education in recent times – and perhaps ever. QAA is, for those who have suffered through its tawdry posturing, a cancer that gnaws at the core of knowledge, value and freedom in education; its carcinogenic growth is now perhaps the greatest pervasive danger to the function of a university as a surviving institution. It has presided over the valorisation and celebration of mediocrity, paradoxically at the very moment when it is allegedly assuring the public of the quality of education and Universities.
>
> (Docherty 2008: 25–6)

This official mutilation would be marginally less objectionable if the QAA itself was a little more careful about its own procedures, but these have been the subject of serious criticism. Cook, Butcher and Raeside (2006) have shown that the subject review grades announced to the sweating staff at the end of a visit, and subsequently used in the university league tables, are dubious to say the least. Yet such grades are of vital importance in the marketplace of education.

Another example is the increasingly bureaucratic processing of students. In most institutions academics are no longer trusted to assess their students fairly and so anonymous marking has been introduced. Empirical evidence has been presented to justify this change and there are good arguments in its favour. However, there have been some less laudable consequences. When students are identified only by numbers it is much more difficult to follow and assist individual students. It is a well-intended innovation which has the unintended effect of de-humanising the activity of teaching. This is especially significant where there are modular degrees in which the great majority of a student's work is assessed and counted towards their passing or failing. A student who has special handicaps, such as when English is not their first language or they have relatively poor language skills, cannot be identified, so it is difficult to make allowance in allocating a mark.

The chilling, mechanical nature of this system is most noticeable in examination boards when the staff assembles to go through the whole list of students and decide on their performance. These meetings used to have the nature of deliberations by those who had taught the students, in which some flexibility was exercised and special circumstances taken into account. There would be lengthy discussions of individual students and their special difficulties. Now, too often, examination boards are cold, mechanical devices for processing students efficiently according to the numbers that have been fed into the office computers, observed by a dumb-show of nodding academics – if any can be persuaded to attend. Anyone who has witnessed this change must surely feel some unease.

Another illustration of the growth and influence of managerialism concerns teaching timetables. In many institutions it was once customary for academics to have substantial power over the organisation of their working environment. Indeed, it was not unusual for one or more of the teaching staff in each faculty or department to have the irksome but necessary task of drawing up the teaching timetable each term. They would request from their teaching colleagues what courses each was designated to teach and what lectures, seminar groups or classes etc., together with student numbers, they thought they would require. Then, in coordination with a central person in charge of room allocation they would draw up a timetable for each teacher.

This method had several advantages. Most particularly, the timetable and room allocation was based on the educational or pedagogic needs of the teachers and students. The duration of sessions would suit the subjects being studied: a science tutor could request a three hour laboratory session to provide time for elaborate experimental work, while a mathematics or philosophy tutor could divide the time into smaller units suitable to their subjects. They could also request rooms that best fitted their activities. Another advantage was that staff could, to some extent, organise their time to suit their individual needs or preferences and those of the students. Someone heavily committed to research could concentrate their teaching on, say, three days a week so as to give them two clear days for research. A tutor with family commitments could ensure that his or her teaching was completed before the time that they must collect children from school, and so on. A similar account could be taken of the needs of students. For example, courses with large numbers of mature students could be timetabled so as to accommodate their family commitments.

Seen through managerial eyes this is an appalling method for producing a timetable. Having sessions differing so enormously in length, staff squabbling over the best rooms, academics or students able to skive off for two days a week, or come and go according to their personal preferences: this is antithetical to any rational scheme of management. The first step in correcting this abomination is to centralise timetabling. It must be done by non-academics in a central office. Individual needs of subject tutors can be presented but the central officers must have the right to ignore or override such requests. Thus the distance between the educational activities – the prime purpose of the college – and the process of timetable design has been increased. Those composing the timetable have little knowledge of the teaching methods required or the kind of rooms that are best suited. Slowly the allocation of time and space is modified to suit a tidy and efficient use of staff and rooms: pedagogic considerations are relegated in importance, and as for the personal convenience of the teaching staff and students, that is given the priority it deserves – very low.

The next step is likely to come with the introduction of a modular degree – to be discussed more fully in the following chapter. Here it only needs to be said that, in a typical modular degree system, students can assemble their degree from a large number of small units or modules. One of the main purposes of a modular degree is to allow the maximum of flexibility and choice for students. Of course, this requires that as many modules as possible are available in as many combinations as possible. In turn this requires that the timetable is spread out over the day and week and that standard time periods are allocated to each module. The result is a timetable designed almost exclusively to suit a managerial system but which pays little respect to the educational activities it controls, or those primarily engaged in those activities – teaching staff and students. Apart from the effect on morale and the disempowerment of both academics and students, this system encourages extensive efforts to subvert the system and ameliorate its worst features.

We have argued that as management changes so it changes what it manages.

Academic staff must not only be accountable for their teaching and research performances, they must ensure that these are measurable – they must provide "indicators" that are checkable by others. This changes at least three things. First, the climate of trust gives way to a climate of doubt; the idea of service gives way to the notions of monitoring, checking and accountability, and the professional ethos is transformed into one of piece-work (Halsey 1992; Winter 1999; Strathern 2000; Wright 2001). A teacher must pursue the goal of producing a programme of studies that can be monitored, whether or not he or she feels that it is the best educational approach. The researcher must publish the required number of papers whether or not he or she feels they have anything worth publishing. Wittgenstein, one of the greatest philosophers of modern times, published one philosophical book and one paper during his life (apart from a dictionary for elementary school children). Today he would have been elbowed over into an administrator's job in a university, although we do not envy the line manager who suggested it to him.

Mass education, the pressures of audit, quality assurance and the need to fit students for employment rather than educate them, have all helped to squeeze out diversity and adventurous teaching, and have diminished the humanity of the institutions and their status as critics of society (Bone and McNay 2006; Docherty 2008). These are profound and damaging changes. Once again they are predominately, but not entirely, a feature of the newer, post-1992, institutions. It is interesting to note that Oxford University has recently repulsed efforts to "modernise" the ancient system by which they are governed, which would have weakened the control of academics over their own institutions and passed it to "professionals". Perhaps it takes 800 years to brew such wisdom, or perhaps it is the solidity of their status that makes them able to resist the erratic breezes of fashion.

Some may feel that it is about time that academics lose their cosy, casual and indulgent ways, and brave the same rigours that most working people have to face, but this is to misjudge both the past and the present. It has always been the case that teaching involves a close, human interaction that is constantly evaluated by those involved, and the products of teaching are eventually measured by the performance of the taught. It is obvious to those affected – the students and other academics – when it is badly done. Similarly, research of any value has to be published in peer-reviewed journals or exposed to an equally demanding and discerning audience in some other way. All that has been added are performance indicators that display the quantity produced or the satisfactory completion of documents, to "generic managers" who can then monitor "production".

It is worth adding that the new system of accountability is open to fabrication and artifice in ways impossible in the real tests that operated previously: it is far easier to fool a bureaucratic system than it is demanding students and well informed colleagues. The time now spent on screwing the system could be better used. What is needed is more rigorous use of monitoring that works, rather than the imposition of another layer that does not. Poor teachers and lazy researchers can easily be identified by those who work with them. What is required is more effective help and, if necessary, coercion, and the best way of providing these is within a proud profession, not a demoralised workforce.

As remarked earlier, research is another area where managerialism is creeping in. As pressure is placed upon universities to be more commercial and make links with industry, so new managerial systems have to be introduced. Business development departments, enterprise and marketing units are proliferating. These demand specialist skills which many academic researchers lack. Hence the need for managers and executives whose expertise – and salaries – must match those in the commercial world. We wonder how long it will be before they begin to direct what research is done, how it is conducted and how, or whether, it is published. Once the research becomes primarily a source of income, rather than a source of knowledge, it will be accountants who decide upon its value.

There is a desperate need to examine, critically, the managerial structures within many of today's institutions of higher education. It is not just the financial cost of the administrative bureaucracies that needs to be pruned. As we have shown, it is primarily the oppressive burden of a top-down hierarchy that, by its sheer weight, distorts what it squats upon. This distortion induces changes in the primary activities of universities: the teaching, learning and research. It is to one important aspect of this that we now turn.

4
Modules and Mutilation

... All new and perfectly unlike his neighbour, ...

Robert Graves, *Welsh Incident*

Management, when it is bad and overbearing, changes what it manages. The new managerial ethos in many universities has changed the nature of the education being offered. In this case it has been aided by the market and consumerist trend discussed below in Chapter 6. Put crudely, these developments have tended to convert education into a commodity. Knowledge, skills and even understanding have to be identified, listed, and divided up into manageable packages: small gobbets called 'modules' that are relatively short, discrete programmes of learning. Each module can then be priced and its delivery monitored. These manageable packages can be accumulated by students who "buy" them at the price demanded by the assessment regime: perhaps an essay or an examination or both, depending on the size of the module.

Modular degrees have become very popular especially in the newer universities and colleges. There were several persuasive arguments in their favour when they were first introduced. It was seen as exactly what we wanted – a way of providing cheap, mass education for a diverse population of students. Modular degrees came together with the Credit Accumulation and Transfer Scheme (CATS) by which each module was given a number of CATS points.

The first advantage was that students could build their degree programme to suit their tastes, talents or needs, because the modular system could allow a wide choice of options. The second advantage was that if the student had to move to another university, they could take their modules and the corresponding points with them and so avoid having to start all over again. A third advantage was that, if a student could not complete their studies for some reason, they would not leave empty handed. Typically, a completed first year would earn them 120 CATS points and they would leave with a Certificate of Higher Education. If the student added a further 120 second level points they could leave with a Diploma in Higher Education, and if they added 180 more third level points they could be awarded a pass degree, while another 60 would give them an honours degree. Underlying these acclaimed advantages was another: modularisation would facilitate the auditing of quality and performance, and this would allow customers to choose between universities (Edwards 1998).

These may be real advantages, and it must be clearly stated that there are good modular degrees around the UK, and there are many people who have benefited immensely by passing through them. For example, the Open University has made particularly good use of a well designed variety of the modular system, which suits its students, and its methods of teaching, admirably. However, the system has serious shortcomings both in practice and in theory. We will discuss some of these shortcomings here and take up others in the next chapter, but we must stress that the corrupting changes with which we are concerned can damage any kind of degree programme: it is just that the effects are seen most starkly in modular degrees. It is worth adding that many students who have worked their way through poorly designed degree programmes triumph despite that handicap, and emerge as educated people: our concern is for those who are less fortunate.

First, the idea that students can build their degrees as they wish by choosing what modules they like, has severe limitations and is very questionable in educational terms. Some of the limitations are practical: cash-strapped universities cannot offer a wide range of options or allow modules to run if chosen by very few students. As mentioned in the previous chapter, constructing a timetable that allows any student to choose any combination of modules is extremely difficult and the result is almost universal inconvenience and inefficiency. The teaching day has to be extended to the annoyance of students and staff, and they find their hours scattered over the week in a way that makes paid employment or child care arrangements much more difficult, at a time when students are forced to seek them. Real "pick and mix" degrees are generally looked on disparagingly by both academics and employers so, in most cases, there is close guidance on what choices a student is allowed. This choice is also constrained by the need to have a coherent path of development through a degree, with first year modules being made prerequisites for second year modules and so on. The result is that choice is often very limited, especially in the smaller colleges, although bigger institutions such as the Open University, with its huge student population, can do the job properly.

Second, the idea that students can switch easily from one institution to another clutching their CATS points is undermined by the need for coherent degree programmes. A university will generally specify, not just what points they require, but what content students must have covered before accepting them on to their degree programme. Furthermore, the number of students who need to switch from one university to another is very small relative to the number that stay at the same institution throughout their degree. For this reason it is highly questionable whether degree programmes should be radically changed to facilitate a small minority, especially as there may be other, less drastic and more effective, ways of doing so.

Third, while the lower qualifications may be given when a student cannot complete their full degree programme, these struggle for recognition and status. This is likely to become an increasing problem as the number of people with degrees reaches almost half the young population. We are likely to reach a situation in which a tick in the 'Do you possess a degree?' box will be a prerequisite for almost all jobs that pay the average wage and above, or which have anything like a career structure attached to them.

Finally, competition for students is a very real aspect of many universities and colleges, especially the less prestigious, but its effects and its usefulness are questionable. The temptations to lower entrance requirements, offer "trendy" degree courses irrespective of either their intrinsic worth or their employment prospects, and to take in students who have little real chance of succeeding, are all too seductive. What is more, many students, especially those from that part of the population now being harvested, have little choice about which institutions will accept them, and not a lot of guidance about how to make even this limited choice. We may add to this the doubt that modular degrees are the best educational approach for less able students; a point to be elaborated in the next chapter.

These practical difficulties are real enough, but there are more serious objections to modularisation. The chief focus of criticism is that it is a major component of the drift towards a *market* view of education and the *commodification* of knowledge, and all that follows from it. A range of scholars have analysed and discussed these problems as they are manifested in education, but so far with little effect (Lyotard 1984; Jameson 1991; Barnett 1994; Edwards 1998; Winter 1999; Brecher 2002; Evans 2004; Brown 2007). The debate concerns not just the fashion for modular courses but a broader move towards seeing education in terms of "competences" and "learning outcomes", topics to which we will return in Chapter 7. The debate is often intertwined with broader philosophical issues, especially the creeping influence of capitalism, the flowering of postmodernism, and the relativist view of knowledge, and we will return to these in Chapter 9. Here it will suffice to lay out the main ideas.

Starting with the obvious, commodification is the process of turning something into a commodity: something that can be bought and sold. Obviously many things, manufactured goods for example, are properly considered to be commodities, but it is widely held that some things, such as people, health care, education, policing services, friendship and so on, cannot be considered in this way or are debased if they are. However, it is equally obvious that at least some of these things can and have been commodified: even people have been bought and sold as slaves, indeed some still are; while health care is a commodity in many countries and, it is argued, higher education is becoming one in Britain.

Exactly what is involved in commodification is a complex and debatable question. Perhaps the best analysis has been given by Margaret Radin (1993; 1996) who has suggested that something has been commodified when it is treated like an object, a thing to be used; when it is not treated as a unique individual but as fungible – that is as if it can be replaced by another without loss; when its value can be placed on a scale for comparison with other goods, and when its value can be expressed in monetary terms. To be a commodity is to be marketable and this involves having a perceived instrumental value; whether because of usefulness, decorative qualities or whatever.

It is also reasonable to debate when and whether commodification is or is not undesirable. Many writers have argued that it can be seriously harmful and that is the position taken by those cited above who oppose the commodification of education. In his excellent discussion of commodification, Steven Lukes (2006) identifies several kinds of attack. The 'corruption argument' claims that something may be debased or distorted by commodification. The 'contamination argument' claims that when one thing is debased by commodification the corruption can spread to related goods or services. However, Lukes feels that such arguments, while not entirely mistaken, are open to criticism: 'To some ears there is more than a hint of paternalism, primness, cultural élitism or else communitarian nostalgia about such arguments . . .' (Lukes 2006: 161). Consequently he formulates two more robust criticisms of inappropriate commodification. He argues that markets can perpetuate or increase inequalities, and they undermine citizenship. Both of these arguments are relevant to education and must be discussed further.

We suggest that there are two main ways in which education can be commodified: as a whole or in the way its parts are delivered. First, considering education as a whole: in Britain education has long been a commodity at primary and secondary levels, since private education and the "public school" system has been available to all those who can afford it. The advantages to those students whose parents can afford a public school education are enormous. As well as the social and employment benefits the most obvious reward is access to the best universities. While only 7 per cent of schools are so-called "public schools", they supply almost 50 per cent of entrants to Oxford and Cambridge universities. Of course Oxbridge insists that it takes in students strictly according to their ability and suitability and, in general, this has become the accepted picture of higher education in Britain. However, examined in detail the picture becomes more complicated. Today the public school entrants to Oxbridge do not, it is true, buy their places, but they do buy what it takes to win them. The major public schools lay enormous emphasis on grooming their students for Oxbridge. Of course they try to ensure that their students get straight As or A-stars at A-level, but they also equip them with the skills, attitudes and confidence required to win entry to the most prestigious institutions. To this can be added the network of connections between the schools and universities: the old boys and old girls.

Given the financial difficulties of UK universities, it is understandable that they should seek to increase the proportion of overseas students, because they can charge them much higher fees than the home-grown specimens. This almost certainly acts as a market mechanism which excludes some would-be home-grown students, especially from the more prestigious universities. Fear has also been expressed about the effect on the standards within our universities of recruiting overseas students. Professor Alison Richard, vice-chancellor of Cambridge University, has warned that, in the competition with other countries such as the United States of America who offer generous financial assistance, we are failing to attract the brightest students. In going for quantity rather than quality we may get into a downward spiral in standards which will affect all students (Garner 2007).

In any case things are changing. Students in England and Wales now have a radically different relationship with their higher education: they purchase it. Loans, grants and bursaries may or may not ameliorate the operations of the market and make differences of income and social class less significant, but what is important here is that obtaining higher education has become increasingly more like purchasing a commodity. A glance at history suggests that the more higher education resembles a market the more likely it is that wealth will buy the best and inequalities will grow, especially as tuition fees soar.

We can speculate that one way in which inequality will manifest itself will be in the kind of university to which students can aspire. As already mentioned, it looks as if there will be two chief groups of higher education institution in Britain: those that retain the traditional mix of teaching and research and those that are almost exclusively teaching institutions. The former will employ the famous names and Nobel Laureates, and will have no difficulty in recruiting the brightest staff – those who want to contribute to their subject and build an impressive list of publications. These universities are likely to be wealthy enough to enhance the pay of their academics according to their performance: a practice that is already underway (Baty 2006a). The tuition fees will rise to whatever future governments allow and only the brightest and most wealthy students will gain entrance. The rest – and that is the large majority – will go to the teaching institutions where the staff will be employed to teach and have little time or support for research. Here mass education will be seen at its most stark. The divide will be as real and permanent for teaching staff as for students, and it will be fully acknowledged more widely; especially by employers. Roger Brown, vice-chancellor of Southampton Solent University (reported in Sanders 2006) has pointed out that steep rises in university fees in the USA have priced out poor students from some institutions, and done little to improve teaching.

The second way in which education can be commodified is in the way its constituent parts are delivered. Here the system of values and prices is not, generally, a monetary one but it can be argued that education is being commodified none the less. For knowledge to be seen as a commodity it must be divided up into recognizable, manageable, pieces or objects, and these must be seen as having a use or decorative value. Each must be priced and available in a market place to be chosen by the customers. On this model, an education will consist of a number of such items of knowledge. The knowledge may be in the form of purported facts or of skills – in Gilbert Ryle's terminology 'knowledge that' or 'knowledge how' (Ryle 1949), but their value lies in their perceived usefulness, not in their truth or because they are intrinsically worthwhile. A modular degree allows knowledge to be offered exactly in this way – as a commodity – and, we claim, encourages a "*consumerist*" attitude to education.

The effect on the student is to encourage an entirely utilitarian attitude towards learning. What matters is not the intrinsic worth of the subject or the satisfaction of gaining understanding, but assembling a qualification. The degree that results may be like a necklace made up of disparate beads 'All new, each perfectly unlike its neighbour . . .' rather than a unified whole. Essays, seminar debates and exercises are not a means to developing knowledge and skills, they are the price that must be paid to tick off the module and get more CATS points. We might say that this approach treats knowledge, indeed education, as fungible. When buying nails it would be bizarre to quarrel with the shop assistant because he or she had selected them randomly from the appropriate box but, when collecting your child from school, it would be understandable to look askance at a teacher who said that, since they had lost your child, you had better take another from the playground. We suggest that knowledge and education are more like children than nails. Specimens of each are unique and have a unique value.

As the philosopher Bob Brecher says in a trenchant polemic against modularity (Brecher 2002: 18):

> Modularity transforms knowledge into a commodity, to be consumed as leisure activity, a matter of gathering and reproducing information: you learn; write up what you have learnt; have it assessed; forget it; and go on to consume the next gobbet.

Of course many students enjoy their time at university and many academics do their best to ensure that they do, but it is often despite the modular systems in which they find themselves. Good, educated students emerge from such institutions, but too many leave with, at best, a kind of disjointed training and at worst a degree certificate listing the topics they visited – lest they should forget even that.

The effect on the teaching staff is that they come to see their task as serving up modules rather than engaging with their students in the exploration of a fascinating subject. They "process" so many students through such a rigid, pre-designed machine that they have no time to do research in their subject and, even if they did, they have no licence to introduce it into the syllabus to freshen and enliven the material. Teaching becomes like a guided tour through an art gallery with only a few seconds to spend at each picture – just enough time to point and walk on. The marking load is enormous because every module must be assessed and there are hordes of students. But it is not that alone that makes the task so onerous; it is also the knowledge that the assessments are entirely aimed at passing or failing the students, not giving help and guidance, not *teaching*: by the time essays or other work is marked and returned the students have moved on to the next module and all but the mark appears irrelevant. The ineffectiveness of entirely summative assessment in encouraging students to study is well known (Gibbs and Dunbar-Goddet 2007) but that is all that time allows.

As Brecher (2002: 18) points out, it is no wonder that the managers of, what he calls "Disneyland universities",

> can rely increasingly on casual labour: self-contained as modules are, there is no need for those who deliver them to be in any way connected with those delivering others, or indeed with anything resembling an intellectual community.

Of course, there are academics who like the modular system and enjoy this way of teaching – although much depends on how it is designed and how well it is run – and those who want part-time work benefit enormously, but overall the consequences for teachers have been dire (Bone and McNay 2006).

The effect of the market ethos on the universities is that they are driven to become competitive corporate enterprises that manufacture the desired commodities. And the commodities that are desired by many students and employers are degree certificates not educations. In a ruthless marketplace, universities must focus on their finances and this will mainly involve ensuring that they can attract students. Their ability to attract students will depend, in large measure, on their standing in the league tables published annually. This will involve such things as inflating the number of first class degrees they award and reducing their failure rates. How such things are achieved is open to question. We must be careful: markets attract barrow boys – slick operators who will sell anything, however dubious, to those gullible or desperate enough to buy.

That "grade inflation" is happening, for whatever reason, is beyond dispute. Over the six years from 1998–99 to 2004–05 the number of first class degrees awarded increased markedly. Over the same period the inflation of "good" honours degrees, that is upper seconds and firsts, was even more noticeable:

now well over half of students achieve these grades (Ramsden 2005). And, once again, these developments are predominantly, but not wholly, a feature of the newer universities.

Universities exist to educate; to seek truth; to contribute to the culture; as sources of critical appraisal of political and social changes, and to enhance human well-being. But these attributes are, at best, secondary matters as far as managers are concerned and, if consumerism is taken seriously, they have no place at all. Of course this is not true of all universities. It is not surprising that Oxford and Cambridge have resisted modularisation, and some of the institutions that embraced it are struggling to return to something better. However, given the need to educate so many more young people, we have to ask what is a better alternative. We will make some suggestions in later chapters.

Before we do so we must explore the recent changes further because it might be argued that all this talk of "consumerism", "commodification" and "marketisation" is beside the point. If the new and more diverse intake of students require different education from that of the élite that preceded them, perhaps we require a new system of pedagogy, and perhaps this is what modularisation plays a part in offering. That is to say, perhaps it lends itself to methods of teaching and learning that suit the new spectrum of students. This is what we discuss in the next chapter.

5
A Thought Experiment

In the previous chapter we saw that modular degrees can be seen as a part of the move towards a market model for higher education, with its commodification of knowledge and managerial dominance. However, it might be argued that, despite these blemishes, modularisation can be justified because it has educational advantages: it has pedagogical merits which make it particularly suited to the needs of the newly expanded intake of students. It might be claimed that it offers the less skilled, less able or less motivated students smaller, less daunting, segments of learning; delivered in such a way as to facilitate their acquisition by even the least proficient. In fact the opposite is true.

To justify this criticism we offer a thought experiment which, although it is both over-simple and unsubtle, none the less raises some important educational issues and throws serious doubt upon the educational value of the modular approach. The experiment involves describing two groups of students and two universities and asks the reader to decide how they would be best matched. This will be followed by some observations of our own.

The first group of students, which we can call Group *A*, is comprised of those that have had a consistently successful school career and have achieved at least three straight As at A-level. They are skilled in studying and understand how to find information, organise their material, produce good essays, sit examinations successfully and do well in several other forms of assessment. Their success has generally given them confidence in themselves and their ability, and left them with a genuine interest in their chosen subjects, a desire to learn more and a liking for study.

Most of Group *A* are highly literate: they read well and widely, and write with sound grammar and an appropriate academic style. There may be some mature students in this group who have not got the same school record or grades at A-level, but they will have been in demanding jobs that require similar skills and will have proved their ability by presenting essays. Many students in this group will have taken it as a matter of course that they will go to university, expecting to do so since childhood. It is more than likely that their parents will be well educated and be very supportive. These students will generally have a fairly clear idea of what they want to study and what careers they wish to pursue.

The second group of students, Group *B*, is comprised of those who have had a rather less successful school career. They have been in the lower or middle streams and have managed, with difficulty, to scrape a modest set of A-level results consisting of Ds, Cs and perhaps a few Bs. They have struggled to master the basic study skills; they have trouble assembling and organising material, their essays are not well written and many of them fear or dislike examinations and most forms of assessment. Their relatively unsuccessful school career has left many of them with a lack of self-confidence, anxiety about failing, no great affection for studying and no marked interest in any subject.

For the most part, Group *B* read infrequently, their vocabulary is relatively poor and they have problems with grammar and paragraph construction. There may be mature students in this group but they will generally be people who have been out of education for at least ten years, doing jobs that make only modest intellectual demands. Many may not have written essays or sat examinations during that interval and admit that they are very anxious about doing so, while a relatively high proportion will have such difficulties as dyslexia. Many of the students in Group *B* will be the first in their family to have gone to university and although their parents may be encouraging there will be little intellectual help. They may be uncertain both about what they want to study and what careers may be open to them. Because of their low A-level grades many may have little choice but to accept what places are offered to them.

So much for the students, now let us consider the universities. University *X* divides the academic year into two semesters and offers a modular degree. Each module is self-contained but may be related to others. Students study at least three, perhaps four, modules simultaneously and each module lasts for one semester. Each module, including those in the first semester of the first year, is assessed by at least two pieces of assessment; typically an essay and an examination. Every piece of assessment from the very first is summative: that is to say it is given a mark or grade which determines whether students pass or fail the module. Thus in each semester, even those of the first year, the students have to undertake about six or eight summative tests. Students must pass almost all modules to obtain a degree. Feedback will be given on some of the assessments, the essays for example, but the assessments will generally be returned to students shortly before they complete the module and move on to another. There is no feedback on the examinations other than pass/fail. There will be little or no formative assessment: that is exercises designed to develop the students' study skills and which do not determine whether students pass or fail. The modular degree offers the students some choices in each semester so that they can, to some extent, design their own programme of study.

University *Y* does not use modules or semesters. Its courses are generally a year long and some may be longer; they are broad in scope and students would normally take only two in parallel. The courses are intended to give an extended and coherent introduction to a subject and to the required study techniques, beginning fairly broadly and becoming more specialised; the students visiting and revisiting the various topics at increasingly higher levels. The students have many formative assessments before they undertake any summative tests. Typically they produce at least one short essay every two weeks, which is commented on almost immediately. These essays are designed to help students develop their study and writing skills as well as their understanding of the subject. Performance in these tasks does not count towards the pass or failure of students but there are summative assessments at the end of the year. There is a relatively small amount of choice of courses but the students can change the direction of their studies at the end of the first year when they have a clearer idea of the subjects involved.

Which group of students is suited to which university? The answer would appear to be obvious. The first group of students, Group *A*, with their straight A grades are suited to University *X*. They are equipped to cope with the demands of summative assessment from the outset and most will face the repeated tests and examination with equanimity. They are able to make informed choices about the modules on offer and equipped to cope with studying several disparate subjects in parallel. The second group, Group *B*, with their modest or poor A-levels and their lack of study skills, will be much better suited to University *Y* with its emphasis on formative assessment and its longer but fewer courses.

It is fairly obvious that exactly the opposite happens in practice. It is also obvious that a much higher percentage of the newly expanded student intake will fall into Group *B* than Group *A* and they will end up in universities of type *X* rather than type *Y*.

The consequences of this mismatch are numerous and damaging. First, a much larger drop-out of students can be predicted from type *X* universities since, from the outset, the students are faced with so many opportunities to fail or do badly, and with very little help to develop the skills they need. In contrast, University *Y* will have much less trouble with retention: its straight A students will enjoy developing an understanding of their subject and improving their academic skills by repeated practice. Sure enough, this difference is there in the statistics. The continuation rate – that is the proportion of those first year students who continue into the second year – varies enormously, from almost 99 per cent at Oxbridge, down to around 82 per cent at such universities as Bolton and Chester (Bourn 2007: 20). Rates of students failing to complete their degrees show a similar pattern. There will almost certainly be other factors that affect these drop-out rates, but it is reasonable to suggest that the course structures, assessment regimes and teaching methods are amongst the most significant.

Second, we should expect that the students at University X will become fixated on the mark or grade they obtain for their essays with the consequence that they will pay little attention to the comments concerning their study skills. Their survival depends on their marks, so what little helpful information they get will be too late and go largely unregarded. They are actively encouraged by the system to ignore the very help they need.

Third, we should expect these students to see their modules as commodities which have to be "bought" at the price of one or two pieces of assessment. Their interest in the modules will tend to be limited to getting what is required to pass. Having obtained the module, it will be of no further significance unless another module is directly linked to it: the student's focus will be on the next hurdle. Typically, the students at University Y will come to value both the discipline and the scholarly activities and they will be more likely to be changed by their education.

The current mismatch has also brought about various measures to try to deal with the difficulties it breeds. For example, the introduction into universities of type X, with its modular degrees, of an academic tutor system to help the students develop their study skills. This has the disadvantage of being an "add-on" provision which runs alongside the student's subject-based studies. It is likely to be seen as an added "burden" unrelated to their numerous subject areas, and attendance is likely to be low, especially amongst those who need it most. Contrast this with the process in universities of type Y in which intensive help with study skills is integrated with their main studies by means of the formative assessment. It is given quickly and is directly relevant to the main tasks being undertaken by the students. How to study the discipline is perceived, by both teacher and taught, as integral to the study of the discipline, not separate.

Because of the very frequent summative assessment in the modular schemes of type X universities, it will appear necessary to introduce various schemes to help the students cope with their essays and exams. Since each assessment will determine whether they pass or fail, it may be felt that they should be given clear guidance about what is expected of them. To this end, the students may be given a detailed list of precise learning outcomes and assured that the assessment will be based directly upon them. They may also be given detailed assessment criteria intended to spell out exactly what the students must do to achieve a pass, and similar stipulations about each of the various grades or percentages. In brief, the students are told, in writing, what will be expected of them and what they have to do to do well. This may sound reasonable but is, in fact, as near nonsense as makes no difference: a claim that will be justified in Chapter 7.

Notice the contrast with the system employed in type *Y* universities where the student acquires an understanding of what is expected by frequent and repeated practice. They face summative assessments only after numerous formative exercises each of which is commented upon. It should be noted that there is evidence that students respond most positively to formative-only assessment and oral feedback from tutors. They respond less well to a diet of much summative assessment and little formative, and least of all to little assessment of either kind (Gibbs 2007; Gibbs and Dunbar-Goddet 2007).

We suggest that this thought experiment illuminates some of the major errors that have accompanied the expansion of higher education. The very laudable project of widening participation is unlikely to increase recruitment from the first group of potential students, Group *A*, who are all very well qualified and equipped for university. The new intake is likely to be from those of the second kind, Group *B*, who have moderate to poor A-levels. Perhaps it is time to try to create the experience of University *Y* in University *X*.

It is claimed that one advantage of a modular system is that students have more choice and can use that to pursue those subjects that they particularly enjoy. This is undoubtedly a virtue. However, there are dangers even in this seemingly benign feature. In addition to those already discussed above, students may lack sufficient knowledge to make rational choices and may choose modules for dubious reasons. They may choose a module because they perceive it to be "easier" than others, or because it does not involve an examination, or because it fits in with their hours of work, or because their friends have chosen it, or because they like the tutor, and so on. Students can systematically avoid subjects that they judge will lower their average grades or involve a lot of work.

While education should not be an exercise in sadism it is necessary that students study what they need for a good education and a sound mastery of a discipline. If they need more practice in examinations it may be advantageous to them to sit more of them. If they are weak in a particular area – say statistics – then they should be encouraged, or even made, to study more of it. Of course a student should be allowed, indeed encouraged, to pursue the subjects they enjoy, but that freedom has to be tempered with a requirement to master the essentials of their chosen discipline.

Choice is important but it can undermine education in another way. One of the important aspects of being a student – and one which echoes the comparison between being a student and being a citizen which will be discussed in the next chapter – is the experience of being part of a group engaged in a common enterprise. This comradeship and feeling of belonging is a vital part of study and one of the main factors in making the transition from novice to expert. Students gain great benefit from feeling that they belong to the community of sociologists, or zoologists, or historians and so on, and they gain enormous support by forming lasting friendships. These important aspects of the student's experience can be impaired if they are constantly shuffled and reshuffled by their choices of modules. Particularly in large institutions, a student may feel alienated and isolated if they pass from one collection of students to another as they take a chain of short courses. They may ameliorate this effect by allowing the choices of their friends to determine what they study, but this may not give them the education they either need or want.

Dividing learning up into modules – particularly if they are of short duration – can have other disadvantages which become apparent in practice. For example, if modules are assessed only by coursework which is set while the module is progressing, students will be tempted to stop attending once they have sufficient material to attempt an essay. There is another practical problem about when to set coursework assignments. If they are set too early, topics will not have been covered by the lectures and seminars and certainly not digested by the students. If assignments are set late in the module, feedback will be given after the module is completed. Short modules also discourage students from buying books or pursuing arduous or expensive research, thus encouraging superficial and transient learning.

These problems present difficulties for those trying to design and teach modular courses. However, there are other problems that are more subtle but which may be even more profound. The modular structure of the course may influence the approach to learning adopted by the students. Specifically, by dividing knowledge into small gobbets, each assessed immediately by perhaps an essay and/or an examination, students may be encouraged to adopt a surface learning technique. Such an approach is generally seen as inappropriate for study at degree level and it is worth discussing why this is.

Surface learning may be defined as the acquisition of largely unrelated facts, opinions, beliefs, abilities and skills, with little attempt to fit them together into a coherent body or connect them to other related knowledge or beliefs (Gibbs 1992). It is superficial in that it does not involve significant understanding, interpretation, integration with related knowledge, or critical evaluation of what has been acquired. A student may adopt a surface learning technique if they perceive that they will be required to merely regurgitate the material but not explain it, draw out its implications, or make connections to a wider field of study beyond the module concerned. Of course, those who design and teach modules may do their best to avoid or ameliorate this problem, but given the modular system and the possibility that the student may not choose certain related modules, this is not an easy task.

It seems fairly self-evident that, at degree level, students should be encouraged to adopt a strategy of deep learning. In deep learning the knowledge, beliefs, abilities and skills are connected together into a coherent view or perspective, and related to what has already been learned. It involves understanding, interpretation and critical evaluation: the student can explain and discuss, not merely repeat, what has been learned, and is capable of generalising and transferring the knowledge and skills to other areas, topics or activities – they have understood certain principles and general concepts as well as particular facts or beliefs. Deep learning is more intellectually demanding, especially for less able students, so there needs to be a clear incentive to adopt it and help to do so. These are not easy to build in to a course consisting of short modules.

Why is this problem important? While some very specific tasks such as mending a fuse or applying lipstick may be quite satisfactory if they remain at the superficial level, it seems reasonable to suggest that deeper learning is generally more desirable and, traditionally, it has been one of the chief goals of higher education. Indeed, it is one of the chief components of a "liberal education". Because of its nature, surface learning will tend to be inert: beyond simply having acquired the learning, the student will be relatively unchanged, for it will play only a trivial and transient part in their life or view of the world. By contrast, deep learning is more likely to be active: it will change or influence the person who possesses it, and be applicable in aspects of their life beyond the original activities by which it was acquired. This will be of great importance to the individual who possesses deep learning because they will be transformed and enriched by it. It will also be of greater benefit than surface learning to prospective employers, because deep learning techniques are eminently transferable to new areas and new tasks. The skills and abilities acquired by deep learning will endure and serve the employer long after specific items of applied knowledge are redundant.

The ideal in higher education has been that learning should be motivated by the intrinsic importance of, and interest in, the subject matter. Deep learning is desirable both because it has greater utility and because, in the long run, it is intrinsically more satisfying and fulfilling to the possessor. It is also likely that surface learning will be quickly lost – as soon as it has served its purpose of passing a module – while deep learning will remain with the student for much longer.

We do not claim that modular degrees *must* encourage surface learning and discourage deep learning. The point is that students, very sensibly, tend to adopt learning strategies that achieve what they perceive to be the best outcomes for them. This instrumental or strategic approach is sensible and understandable – especially when you are paying for your degree. It is the task of the educators to encourage a deep strategy rather than a surface one. If the student sees that he or she will have to study a small area of a subject and face immediate summative assessment, with questions more or less designed to cover the learning outcomes listed for the module, then they will be likely to resort to surface learning. Tough minded students who have a well informed understanding of what constitutes an education may resist these temptations, but the weaker or less confident student is likely to be coaxed or tempted into surface learning, even when they appreciate its shortcomings.

One reason why the modular system of higher education was introduced was because it was seen as a way of educating large numbers of students more "efficiently" – that is to say at less expense and with fewer teaching staff. We have argued that practice has shown this to be seriously mistaken – even if the problems are more evident to the teaching staff than those who manage them. Another reason for its introduction was that it was thought to be a better and more effective educational method than those traditionally used, particularly for students in the newly expanded intake, who might have lesser or different abilities and attitudes. We conclude that this claim is equally ill founded.

However, there is another feature of modularisation that is harmful: it is a major factor in encouraging a "consumerist" attitude in education. It is part of the subtle change in higher education which is encouraging students to see themselves as customers, tutors to see themselves as shopkeepers and universities to act as retail outlets. This is the subject of the next chapter.

6
Students as Customers

To found a great empire for the sole purpose of raising up a people of customers, may at first sight appear a project fit only for a nation of shopkeepers. It is, however, a project altogether unfit for a nation of shopkeepers; but extremely fit for a nation whose government is influenced by shopkeepers.

Adam Smith (1991: 1776) *Wealth of Nations*. Vol. 2: 110

The rise of consumerism within education has had several effects but none have been more significant than those upon the students and their relationship to their universities and their teachers. Against a background of an increasingly commercial and consumer-dominated culture, the provision of free higher education has been abandoned along with most maintenance grants. Many reasons were given for this, some more convincing than others, but the consequences were not fully appreciated. Now students enter education knowing that they are going to have to pay for it. They expect to take up loans and build up considerable debts in pursuit of a qualification that is getting more common by the year.

It has been estimated that students graduating in 2010 can expect to owe £17,500, and some over £20,000 (Push 2008). The result is that students have to focus on getting money. The great majority of students now come from families with modest means, so they have to work to finance themselves. They take up what employment they can in and around the university. For the most part it is unstimulating, mundane and low-paid work, while it is reported that some even resort to prostitution (Milne 2006).

A survey has shown that less privileged students, such as single parents, mature students and those from lower-income families, tend to be most concerned about getting into debt and are the most likely to work during term time, yet still have the highest level of debt (Brennan, Duaso, Little, Callender and Van Dyke 2005). It showed that 69 per cent struggled to meet financial commitments and 12 per cent were seriously behind with payments. It also suggested that there is a negative relationship between working during term-time and educational attainment, including the final degree result, which supports a previous finding concerning students in Northumbria University (Hunt, Lincoln and Walker 2004). Research reveals a similar deleterious effect amongst American students (Plant, Ericsson, Hill and Asberg 2004). These findings fit only too neatly into the scene described by Wilkinson and Pickett (2009) concerning the effects of inequality on education.

It is a significant consequence of these changes that students have come to see themselves as *customers*. Increasingly their perception is that they are buying a product. This encourages an *instrumental* view of education: its value lies not in itself but in what it can be used to gain. An education that has to be purchased at great expense is purchased for a purpose, and that purpose is what it will earn. At the very least it must pay for itself. What that education contains and whether it is a coherent whole or just a collection of disparate pieces, does not matter, or at least the student will have difficulty in under-standing why it does. What matters to the potential customer is the possession of a qualification – a ticket to a better material standard of living. Knowledge, understanding and all the skills involved in critical thinking and analysis are valuable as a means to something else – gaining an income – a feeling heavily underlined by the huge debt that is acquired while studying. Some students may have a more high minded desire to become educated, but there remains the feeling that this is to be obtained in much the same way as someone might buy a car or washing machine.

As customers, students are now much more like their school friends who went straight out to work. When most students lived on a maintenance grant and had their tuition fees paid by the government there was a distinct condi-tion of "being a student". For most it was a state of communal and voluntary poverty in which a combination of study and "student life" gave them identity and differentiated them from those who were in full-time employment. A couple of decades ago it was a widespread practice that students who wanted to work had to get permission from their tutors; now students regularly fit in their studies between time spent in paid employment. They are working people who happen to study. It is not surprising if they expect the same consumer goods – clothes, mobile phones and the like – that others of their age group enjoy. Nor is it surprising if they see their education as just another purchasable product.

It may be argued that there are some advantages in students seeing them-selves as customers and that there are many areas in which the attitude of a customer is legitimate. Students as customers may be less willing to tolerate a shoddy "product": less willing to suffer poor teaching, sub-standard facilities, under-stocked libraries and appalling accommodation. If students are to seek work, then their timetables must permit them to do so. Timetables must be produced in plenty of time and designed to facilitate employment and child-care, so that working and mature students can organise their lives. The customers may reasonably demand that marking is done fairly and within a specified time, and that the feedback is of the right standard – although, as we have seen, what is actually demanded is not always what ought to be. So, in general, it is not implausible to claim that students as customers will, to use today's popular catch-phrase, drive up standards among universities.

However, it is significant that this has happened just as universities and colleges were becoming increasingly starved of the funds to provide the quality and quantity of academic support for students. As mentioned earlier, student:staff ratios have risen in recent years to levels higher than those in secondary schools, and one-to-one tutorials are a luxury rare indeed outside Oxford and Cambridge. Lecture audiences have increased enormously and many seminars have swollen, rendering their purposes impossible to achieve and turning them into lectures. The sheer quantity of marking and the number of assessments means that feedback is often delayed and perfunctory. Formative feedback suffers most of all. International comparisons show just how far we have moved in these directions (Sastry and Bekhradnia 2007).

For students, individual contact with academic staff has also become a rare luxury in many institutions, and keeping a check on attendance is increasingly difficult. Many universities have introduced elaborate student welfare systems, but these are even further from direct contact with students than the harassed teaching staff. This is almost certainly one of the reasons for student discontent and drop-out but, fortunately for those responsible for this situation, each intake of students has little knowledge of what previous cohorts enjoyed. It may well be that it is only this ignorance of what had gone before that has avoided more serious student unrest. In brief, if students are to see themselves as customers it is reasonable to demand that colleges are given the resources to answer this challenge.

The effect of students acting as customers may have even more far-reaching consequences, whether or not universities have the resources to meet their demands. As the world has recently learned, a market is a capricious beast which will follow short term demands and fads, and go its own way irrespective of longer term consequences. As Steven Lukes (2006) has argued, it can emphasise old inequalities and differences and create yet more.

For example, it may bring about a change to two-year long, or even shorter, degree courses as the most common pattern. Given the high cost of studying, loss of income and the cost of accommodation, it is likely that potential students will see shorter courses as being very attractive. They could reduce the price of a degree by almost a third. It is at least questionable whether two years crammed with unremitting study can give the same quality of education as a longer programme interspersed with time for reflection and wider reading, and it will certainly be a very different experience. However, if the possession of a degree, rather than an education, becomes a routine requirement for employment, the temptation to get it over with in the shortest and least expensive way possible may prove decisive. Once again it seems likely that we shall see emerge a significant difference in educational experience on the basis of wealth, social class and ethnic origin. Since the universities offering two-year degree programmes are unlikely to be those that have a large and lively research culture, this will add to an increasing divide between kinds of higher education. Whether students as customers will be aware of this divide and, more to the point, whether most of them will be in a position to have a real choice between one or the other kind, is another matter.

As mentioned previously, students in English universities already have a raw deal concerning the tuition they receive: international comparisons are striking. In Germany and Austria a first degree generally requires almost seven years of study; in Portugal and Finland the figure is six years, while in Spain and The Netherlands students take an average of just over five. The average in England and Wales is just over three years (Sastry and Bekhradnia 2007). A comparison of the hours spent studying each week is just as remarkable. The figures vary considerably between subjects and between institutions, but the average scheduled hours of teaching in English universities is 14 hours per week, while the total work load – that is teaching time plus private study – is 26 hours per week. This compares with 41 hours in Portugal, 35 in France, 34 in The Netherlands and 29 in Spain (Sastry and Bekhradnia 2007). While differences in the nature of the final qualifications, the entry requirements, the quality and pattern of teaching, length of semesters or terms and so on, make exact comparisons difficult, it is clear that students in English universities are not the most fortunate in Europe.

It is possible that a market approach to higher education may eventually have another consequence: higher education institutions distinguished on cultural, religious and racial grounds. Already several towns and cities have *de facto* racial and religious segregation at primary school level, and the current enthusiasm for faith-based secondary schools and city academies is likely to accelerate the trend at the secondary level. If parents have chosen to guide their children through a favoured kind of school at primary and secondary level, there may well be customer demand for similar provision at the tertiary level. Already there are anxieties about the long term social effects of the present segregation and such worries can only grow as it extends even further. A comparison with the situation that helped cause so much trouble in Northern Ireland is not unreasonable.

There are areas in which the "customer" analogy is simply inappropriate and even damaging. If we examine the notions of customer and student more carefully it becomes evident that there are fundamental differences between them that are of the greatest significance in higher education. In a free market consumer economy, customers are seen as rational individuals who have certain needs, wants and whims and who set out to satisfy them by acquiring the means of purchasing whatever products seem to them to be desirable. The customers compete with others to accumulate the necessary wealth and the producers and providers compete with each other for their custom. It is not the shopkeeper's role, nor is it in his interest, to question the customer's tastes or challenge their choices. For many goods the customers need little knowledge or expertise to make their rational choices, but for some they need expert advice. In such circumstances the shopkeeper is under an obligation not to deceive, but cannot be expected to be so generous with advice that he loses the sale.

There are important differences in the case of a student who sets out to "purchase" either a qualification or, more idealistically, an education. These differences make the use of the term "customer" inappropriate. To start with, unlike a washing machine, the "product" does not exist at the point of purchase. Indeed, it may never exist, because unless the student has the necessary ability and works sufficiently hard they may get neither an education nor a qualification. In this respect being a student is more like being a gardener than a customer, since a gardener may desire to grow superb leeks but will not succeed in doing so unless they apply themselves in the right way.

Furthermore, the student is beholden to the educational expert in a way that is far more fundamental than that of the customer to the salesman. It is precisely the role of the academics to question the student's tastes and challenge their choices. The academic decides what is to constitute the "product" under negotiation. Its content and the level of the material are dictated by the prevailing standards of the discipline concerned. What constitutes a proper degree in, say, history or physics is determined by the current state of those disciplines, as judged by those who are authorities within them. The academics may advertise the broad content of a degree but the student is rarely in a position to dispute this or make an appropriate judgement of it. In modular degrees there is often more choice for the student than was traditionally the case but, even then, the choices are generally made under the constraints of a degree programme and guidance from the teaching staff. "Pick and mix" degrees may be available in some institutions but students find that, if they indulge their whims too much, higher level education and some areas of employment are closed to them.

The students also have a relationship with their teachers which is very different from that which a customer has with the producer of a commodity or the provider of a service. One of the most serious consequences of students seeing themselves as customers is that it distorts the relationship between them and their tutors. We will touch on this topic in later chapters but here we will point out that it is, and ought to be, the academics who decide on what contribution is to be expected from the students and who judge the quality and quantity of the student's performance. The academic is not in the position of a salesperson who has to accept that, at least in principle, the customer is always right. Tutors can be expected to do a competent job at tutoring, but they cannot, and should not, meet every demand of their students; indeed it is their role to insist on greater effort and application if they are lacking.

Academics must be able to forbid, and take disciplinary action against, plagiarism and other forms of cheating without fear of the litigation that a "customer" attitude may encourage (Baty 2006b). There may be increasing pressure on colleges to give the student some influence over their assessment and this may be particularly useful in formative tasks, but to the degree that this allows them to judge the quality of their performance, so the qualification will become less valuable and the assessment more pointless. For this reason it is inevitable that complaint procedures in higher education must make it very difficult for students to pass where they have been failed, increase their marks or improve the grade of their final degree. Mistakes may be made, so there must be mechanisms of reparation, but they ought not to become slot machines for dispensing degree certificates.

Because, properly understood, an education is not a "thing" or "commodity" on display to the public like a piece of furniture in a shop window, the student cannot know what he or she is "purchasing", even when given a detailed description by those who went before. Education is a complex series of experiences; it involves interaction with others and with ideas, artefacts and processes, and these have to be experienced to be appreciated and understood. They cannot be seen while casually window shopping for a qualification. Often what is not greatly valued initially will, with experience and time, come to be conceived of as being significant and a positive contribution to the individual's success and happiness. Each new intake of students is inevitably ignorant of what they are about to undertake in a way that is not true of someone buying, say, a new car or even a holiday, and each intake will have unique experiences depending on the cohort, changes in the educational institution and developments in the subject they are studying.

A proper education at university level does not just consist of giving knowledge or even understanding. This may be true in secondary education where, often driven by the need to shepherd children through numerous tests, the teacher has succeeded when the pupils can repeat what he or she has told them. But at the higher level, the tutor has succeeded when the students question what they are told. Critical analysis and questioning are central to a university education, so the end "product" is not a collection of packages of knowledge but a way of treating such offerings. For this reason an education is not a collection of commodities, it is more like an attitude to life. Ideally, the student achieves the kind of "liberal education" defined in the Preface.

It is important to notice that competition cannot work in the same way within higher education as it does in the consumer marketplace. Ultimately, in the absence of cartels and monopolies, producers and retailers of consumer products must satisfy their customers, however unreasonable are their demands, or be out-performed by their competitors. Manipulative advertising and misinformation may distort this somewhat but the basic picture remains. However, in education, competing institutions cannot make many of the changes that their "customers" may desire. They can improve facilities, engage better teachers and so on, but such things as reducing standards, excluding difficult material, and reducing the burden of assessment, not only make them vulnerable to censure, but are ultimately self-defeating because it reduces the value of what the student achieves.

Some colleges have reduced their entry requirements to entice in more students but there are disadvantages in doing so: the burden on the institution can increase if the students lack the usual skills and abilities, and the league tables will show if the number of completions and the levels of achievement fall. But again, these practical difficulties are less important than the central point: ultimately, the purpose of a higher educational institution is not to satisfy its customers but to give them a good education, and that is not to be judged primarily by the customer (Hart 1997). It may be that in the long run the whole community must decide what constitutes a good education, but that task cannot and ought not to be given to the "customer" at point of purchase.

Finally, there are deeper reasons for resisting the commodification of education: those developed by Steven Lukes from the ideas of T. H. Marshall (Lukes 2006). Lukes argues that when the market is introduced into certain areas of social life, such as education, health care, and support for the ill and unemployed, it can do serious harm: more specifically it can undermine citizenship. Lukes suggests that the market can harm the domain of citizenship in two principal ways and he is worth quoting at length:

> One is the severing of the link between representative (national or local) and citizen and elector (who becomes a customer and consumer). Marketization and public–private partnerships enable politicians to divest themselves of responsibility and, crucially, of accountability for the provision of public services. The government contracts with the supplier but citizens can no longer hold their representatives accountable for service delivery, which is rendered faceless by being consigned to the anonymous forces of the market. Meanwhile governmental agencies such as local education offices in the UK and the Federal Emergency Management Association in the USA become hollowed out and marginalized. The other harm concerns not merely the preconditions of citizenship but those of *good* citizenship – namely, the services that generate and sustain people's capacity to function as good citizens. There is no reason to think that these will be provided by market forces alone to a sufficient extent and in adequate breadth and depth. In particular, when markets invade the spheres of educational provision and public

broadcasting, some of the capacities – notably the cognitive capacity to process information and achieve a rational understanding of one's world – are, to say the least, not encouraged.

(Lukes 2006: 165–66. Italics in the original)

These arguments clearly apply to the commodification of education as a whole, and they are, we believe, a perceptive and timely warning of the eventual effects of present trends.

However, we suggest that there is another level at which Lukes' arguments can be applied. A student's relationship to a university is, or should be, more like that of a citizen to a state than a customer to a supermarket. There are rights and duties on both sides, and loyalty and service on both sides too. The whole institution depends on a mutual engagement in activities beneficial to all and knitted together by trust: albeit trust that is backed up by sanctions and penalties. A reasonable level of education is essential to function as a citizen and everyone should feel that they have equal rights to learning, and that only relevant educational reasons should limit their progress, not their ability to pay. In return the universities can expect students not to squander expensive resources supplied by society. Turning this into a commercial transaction conducted in a marketplace has been a political folly which will tend to undermine proper education and may become a social cancer.

Thus we claim that the market ethos in education transforms the relationship between the individual and society. If a customer purchases a commodity with their own cash they owe no obligation to anyone else, but if a student is given an education by the society in which they live, they have an obligation to that society or, at the very least, they have something to be grateful for. By sharing in a co-operative activity and benefiting from it, they are bound into a community and they may be motivated towards enhancing it. After purchasing a pair of socks a customer has no obligation to the shop.

Putting these arguments together, it is plausible to see that the growth of managerialism and a consumerist and market ethos is producing important and dangerous changes in our educational system. These changes, including the proliferation of modular degrees, stand accused of undermining the traditional liberal view of education as something of value in itself – something that transforms those who possess it. They also undermine the idea of a university as a place that seeks to discover and transmit truth and foster critical thinking. They encourage students to assemble a degree like a bird-watcher ticking off species, where coherence and deep understanding are neglected in favour of a disjointed aggregation of items. The final quality of the degree is measured by performance in the various modules and may not consider how, or whether, these units are welded together into a coherent whole. The final value of the degree is what it will purchase in the job market – and, for many, that may turn out to be remarkably little.

We hope that the topics discussed so far, such as managerialism, commodification of knowledge, modularisation, consumerism and so on, are not seen as abstract or at a level removed from the practical activities that go on within universities. We have tried to show that they are, in fact, very practical matters that have a serious impact on both teachers and taught. To emphasise our thesis, in the next chapter we will discuss a very practical matter which will illustrate just how damaging practices can be when they are "encouraged" by powerful forces. Fads and fashions are inevitable in any human activity but, like five-inch heels, they are not always a good thing.

7
Auditing Learning

'When I use a word,' Humpty Dumpty said in a rather scornful tone, 'it means just what I choose it to mean, – neither more nor less.'
Lewis Carroll (1965: 1871) *Through the Looking-glass*: 174

We have argued that the kind of over-management which has insinuated its way into many universities has caused serious problems and consumed too great a proportion of the resources. We also claimed that it eventually begins to change what it manages for its own purposes to the detriment of education. We have given some examples but, in this chapter, we want to illustrate this process in more detail with the sad story of *learning outcomes*. This may seem a rather marginal or esoteric issue but not only is it a vivid illustration, it concerns issues near the heart of teaching and learning.

Learning outcomes, seen as statements of what should be achieved during a teaching session, belong to a family of ideas which include such things as aims, objectives, goals, purposes, hopes and aspirations. Such concepts apply wherever we engage in purposeful activity. After all, it seems eminently sensible to think about what you are going to do before doing it and, if others are involved in a joint enterprise, let them know as well.

In the case of teaching, it is wise to decide what we want our students to learn and it seems just as prudent to let the students in on the secret. Consequently, most teachers plan their teaching sessions and try to identify what they hope to achieve. At the beginning of the session they will generally state this as clearly as they can to the students. University tutors might say such things as 'By the end of this morning you will be able to calculate the deflection of a simply supported beam under both static and dynamic loads'; 'In this seminar you will identify the main reasons why the landed aristocracy generally opposed the repeal of the Corn Laws'; or 'In this lecture I shall explain why I believe Professor Michael Dummett has exaggerated the influence of Frege on the development of analytic philosophy', and so on.

Obviously, primary school teachers will be a little less ambitious, but they too will tell the children what is to be learned.

Back in the 1960s, when the great expansion of higher education was just beginning and drawing in increasing amounts of government spending, there was a feeling that educators needed to make their practices more "scientific" and accountable. Very roughly, the perception was that, while educators might know their subjects, they had only a vague idea of the nature of education and an intuitive understanding of the processes of teaching and learning. Presumably they had aims or goals in what they did, but these were, at best, implicit and unformulated. Similarly, the means of assessing the outcomes of their educational activities were determined more by tradition than by any rational design. The justification given for the whole or any part of the social practice of education, if any was given at all, generally amounted to little more than a subjective feeling that we were doing things about right. In the universities, venerable dons knew their subjects and could distinguish, with exquisite nicety, between a beta plus and a beta double plus on a 'Finals' script, but they were somewhat woolly about how they did it.

The feeling amongst the reformers was not necessarily that present educators were doing a bad job, but that the whole process was so poorly understood that it was impossible to develop and manage it in a rational way. Clearly, if huge amounts of money were to be poured into the burgeoning education system, things had to change.

In retrospect it is possible to discern three main aims of the movement towards reform and modernisation: (1) to make precise and clear what was vague and woolly; (2) to make explicit what was implicit, and (3) to offer objective, measurable criteria where there had been only subjective intuitions. We can see that these were laudable aims – so long as the overarching goal was to improve the practices of education, and not *merely* to make it more manageable.

Educational theorists and philosophers took up the debate. Some focused on such high level topics as the concept of education and the nature of the educated person (Peters 1966, 1967; Dearden, Hirst and Peters 1972) while others discussed the concept of an aim and the formulation of educational aims (Dearden 1968; Langford 1968). For the most part, these early discussions were concerned with such aims as that of developing the educated person, meeting the needs and promoting the interests of the child, and so on. However, it was soon recognised that such broad topics, important though they were, could not offer guidance to those who stood in front of students. Hirst and Peters (1970) stressed the difference between aims and ideals, and between the aims *of* education and aims *in* education. It was one thing to engage in high level philosophical justifications of education and quite another to say what we should be trying to do in classrooms and lecture halls.

In a further move towards clearer guidance, it became widely argued that the educator must be able to distinguish between aims and objectives. Writing in the late 1960s, Hirst spelt out the new programme:

> Not long ago educationalists talked about 'aims' rather than 'objectives' and this shift to a more technical term alone indicates a growing aware-ness that more detailed description of the achievements we are after is desirable. If what it is we want to achieve is first indicated in expressions of great generality, these need to be unpacked into more specific terms or little positive guidance is provided for educational practice.
>
> (Hirst 1974: 16)

This distinction soon became orthodoxy. By the 1970s, anyone engaged in designing a degree programme and trying to get it past the Council for National Academic Awards (a predecessor of the QAA) had to know their aims from their objectives or face failure. Hours were spent in getting the documents just right. To what extent all this helped practising teachers is hard to tell, but it became the fashion of the day, along with such things as 'conceptual underpinnings' and 'overarching coherence'.

Debates developed about just what could count as an objective and how a teacher could determine whether they had been achieved. The early work of Bloom, Engelhart, Furst, Hill and Krathwohl (1956), which categorized edu-cational objectives, became widely used and debated as a means of achieving greater specificity. Advocates of precision, following the work of Tyler (1949), argued that objectives should be pre-specified and suited to quantitative measurement. They preferred behavioural objectives: clear statements of what a student would be able to *do* when learning was achieved. These behavioural responses could be verbal or physical movements, and they would be specific and measurable.

Critics argued that such behavioural objectives were of limited use and not a comprehensive solution to the problem of specifying and measuring desirable learning. There might be some use for them in primary schools but they become increasingly implausible as we climb the educational staircase. Perhaps 'The child will be able to do up the buttons on his or her coat' is an acceptable objective in a reception class, but quite what the equivalent would be in a course on semiotics or quantum chromodynamics is difficult to envisage – although the more despairing of academics might think that the same objective would still be pertinent.

One objection to aims and objectives was that, while we might specify them with laudable exactness, they still seemed to be tainted with subjectivity. They could be interpreted in terms of the intentions of educators: statements of what teachers want, hope or aspire to achieve. What was needed was a means of specifying the observable products of educational activities with precision, but which were broader, more flexible and realistic, than behavioural objectives.

Enter *learning outcomes*. These can be seen as the products of the learning process within the pupil (Gagne 1974; Ing 1978). Our objectives as teachers can be identified with our *intended* learning outcomes, but what we observe in the subsequent assessment of our students are *actual* learning outcomes. We must state our intended learning outcomes before we start teaching and use them to formulate our assessments – examinations, practical tests, essay questions and so forth. What the students actually produce in this assessment are the actual learning outcomes.

However, further refinement is needed. We must find a way of specifying learning outcomes with sufficient precision. Furthermore, like the objectives before them, learning outcomes must differ according to the level of teaching and learning concerned. As we have seen, what is appropriate at primary school is quite different from what is required at university. It seems equally obvious that what is appropriate in the first year of a degree is different from that in the second year and so on. It will also be necessary to be able to distinguish between the different grades: As, Bs, Cs, Ds and failure. What is more, it is important that all of this must be achieved in a way that can be shared by all schools or all universities: there must be uniformity to ensure comparable results.

The solution to these problems was to devise a shared language: a vocabu-lary of precise descriptive terms, or 'descriptors', with which to specify the learning outcomes. For example, we might specify that at one level the child or student must be able to describe, recall, name and repeat; while at the next they must be able to define, comprehend, understand and explain; while at the third level they must be able to analyse, evaluate, criticise, compare, integrate, organise, infer and deduce. Once everyone has learnt this special vocabulary and the rules for its use in formulating learning outcomes, we have Nirvana.

Little wonder that learning outcomes came to be favoured amongst edu-cational theorists and began to feature prominently in the guidance of school inspectors, and the Quality As urance Agency (QAA) at university level (Moon 1999). A new fashion had arrived and everyone was going to wear it whether it fitted or not. There were other items in this fashion parade – transferable skills, subject specific and generic outcomes etc. – but 'learning outcomes' were the centrepiece.

Very soon the auditors impressed upon universities that they must pepper their paperwork with the right terminology. Not only must teachers list their intended learning outcomes for each and every teaching session, these must correspond to the learning outcomes enumerated in the booklet for each module, and these in turn must cohere with the learning outcomes listed in the documents describing the whole degree course. It hardly needs adding that all must be written in the language of precise descriptors. But this is not all: the teachers and academics must demonstrate how their assessment scheme exactly tests the extent to which the learning outcomes have been achieved by the students. The students must also understand precisely what is expected of them, so they must be given 'assessment criteria' which exactly reflect the learning outcomes of their modules. The result is a most perfect paper trail leading up, down and round about, ornamented by diagrams with more arrows than Agincourt.

Some individuals have spoken out (e.g. Atherton 2006; Docherty 2008) but we know of no independent survey of the attitudes of academics specifically towards learning outcomes. However, anecdotal evidence makes us confident in claiming that they do not share the enthusiasm of auditors such as the QAA. In designing a module or course, most will list the contents – the topics to be covered – specify the level (e.g. first year degree, master's degree etc.), indicate the books and journals to be used, suggest the teaching methods, time allocation and method of assessment, but will only list learning outcomes if required to do so, and then with a groan. We hope to show that this is not just because of the labour involved. There are better reasons for groaning.

However, in 2007 the QAA produced a report entitled '*Outcomes from Institutional Audit: The Adoption and Use of Learning Outcomes*'. This is based on audits of 70 institutions and is quite ecstatic about its success in promoting the adoption of learning outcomes. In the summary it says:

> It is clear . . . that the inclusion of programme specifications as a key element in the Academic Infrastructure has served to embed the use of learning outcomes across UK higher education programmes.
>
> Almost all of the institutional audit reports published by November 2004 explicitly mention learning outcomes . . . . Sometimes the reports refer to programme outcomes, sometimes to module/unit outcomes, most often they refer to both.
>
> [. . .]
>
> In general, the results of the discipline audit trails show compellingly that most departments in most institutions, have fully adopted the principles of programme design with respect to learning outcomes.
>
> (QAA 2007: 1)

Is this surprising? The QAA is a formidable auditing body with the power to do serious hurt to any institution it judges to be out of line. The grade or rating it gives any department is considered a public record of the quality of its work. If the QAA insists that universities spray their activities with the colour of learning outcomes, then it is not surprising that that is the colour reflected back to them. Academics may groan but they soon learn to describe what they do in the requisite language. They have little choice.

So what is wrong with the learning outcomes fad? In brief, teachers have been forced – and that is the appropriate word – to take a perfectly useful idea and misuse it to the point that it has distorted what they do and made the term virtually meaningless. It is worth explaining why this is so and why it matters (Hussey and Smith 2002; 2008).

First recall that in Lewis Carroll's *Through the Looking-glass*, when Humpty Dumpty said, in a rather scornful tone: 'When I use a word it means just what I choose it to mean, – neither more nor less', Alice replied: 'The question is, whether you *can* make words mean so many different things.' We are with Alice here. If a word or words are used too loosely they forfeit their meaning and become useless.

The term 'learning outcome' has been lifted from its original home – a statement of what was to be learned from a teaching session such as a lecture or seminar – and used to specify what amounts to the contents of a whole module or unit covering many weeks of study; then to refer to what is to be tested by an assessment system, and then to describe what is the intended outcome of an entire degree programme. Clearly, it does not mean the same in each case and the connections between them all are complex (Hussey and Smith 2008). However, the damage done here is relatively slight: if academics have to churn out an audit trail, and if they can make it seem inosculated and coherent by misusing a few words, who cares? Certainly not the auditors. But the fashion has more sinister features: it can damage education.

When used properly, learning outcomes are a sensible and effective part of teaching and learning, as we will show in the following chapter, but they have been hijacked by the auditors and turned into a device for monitoring the performance of teachers. Once the learning outcomes have been stated with the prescribed precision and connected to the assessment method in the correct way, the performance of both teachers and taught can be monitored, even by a "generic manager". Or so the story goes.

The first problem with precise and determinate learning outcomes is that their precision and determinateness are illusory (Hussey and Smith 2002). Even if they are simple descriptions of behavioural responses such as 'will be able to recite the twelve times table' or 'will be able to climb a rope' these things can be done well or badly. The table can be recited falteringly, without understanding and the rope can be climbed inefficiently, with an enormous waste of energy. As soon as we consider more ambitious learning outcomes such as 'the students will understand the structure of DNA' or 'the students will be able to distinguish between metaphors, analogies and similes', or 'the students will be able to critically assess the evidence for the operation of natural selection upon the moth *Biston betularia* in areas affected by industrial pollution' the problem of precision becomes even more obvious.

The apparent precision of such statements as 'students will understand the distinction between artificial and natural selection' depends on the fact that we interpret them in the light of our understanding of the context. What this example would mean in A-level biology and what it would mean at degree level are quite different. The level of understanding depends on the general level of the course of study; on what the students have been, and will be, expected to read; on the depth of discussion in lectures or seminars, and so on. If we add such phrases as 'have a *thorough* understanding . . .' they still have to be interpreted against the educational background: what is thorough at one level is superficial at another. If a student wrote 'natural selection is when the organism's survival depends on nature while in artificial selection it depends on human choice' this would, on the face of it, satisfy the above learning outcome, but while a tutor might find it an acceptable, if unimpressive, answer in secondary school, he or she would think it inadequate in a university. The tutor would do this not because of the precise wording of the learning outcome, but because he or she would have implicit standards of what constitutes an acceptable answer in a specific pedagogical context.

Similar arguments apply whether we are concerned with knowing, understanding or critically analysing: each of these mean different things at different levels. What counts as knowing French grammar, understanding nuclear fission, or what is involved in analysing Philip Larkin's *The Whitsun Weddings*, depends overwhelmingly upon the level and nature of the course of study. The same point applies in learning crafts, dance, music or whatever. Both the students and their teachers have to gain a sense of the appropriate levels of skill and performance from what is generally accepted at the level involved. A boy or girl may get top marks for an "excellent" dovetail joint, but a craftsman might be ashamed of producing a similar specimen. However contrived the wording, learning outcomes only specify what is to be learned if we interpret them correctly according to the context: their "precision" is a sham.

The charade of precision might be tolerable if the fad for specifying learning outcomes had no educational dangers, but it has. First, rules about what is appropriate at different stages of learning can be insensitive to differences between disciplines. There may be subjects in which students can be taught to know at one stage, understand at the next and critically evaluate and analyse at the next, but quite what knowing would be without understanding, and what the latter could be without some degree of analysis, is difficult to envisage. It is not easy to think of an example where such stages could apply. Surely a study of English literature would require all three even at an early stage, and in philosophy if students did not critically evaluate from the start they would not be doing philosophy. Even in the sciences, where there is an awful lot to know and understand, we would not object to 'understanding' even at the highest level. To understand M-theory (a development of string theory) in physics or the Kolyvagin-Flach method in mathematics, are worthy aims in the final year of a degree, even if critical evaluation is a little tentative.

As we will see in the next chapter, the idea that the process of learning is a linear progression through neatly circumscribed stages is simply mistaken. Students need to visit and revisit concepts, theories, bodies of knowledge, skills and ideas many times before they can claim to be educated in respect of them. It may be useful to be told what to expect from a learning session but contrived formulations of outcomes is not the way to do so. The sessions themselves will establish what skills and levels are required of the students. Similarly, it may help a student to be told that their essay is too descriptive and needs to be more critical, but what counts as being more critical depends on what is appropriate or generally agreed at that level. It will be indicated to the student by a skilled teacher, by the recommended reading and by the performance of the other students, not by carefully worded learning outcomes.

A second educational danger associated with stipulated learning outcomes is that they may stifle good teaching. As we explore in the next chapter, it is essential that teachers are flexible and tolerant in the path taken by a teaching and learning session. They must be willing to take up ideas, examples and arguments that emerge from the students, even when this delays or modifies the teacher's original plan for the session. At least in higher education it is not unreasonable to allow students themselves to choose some of the objectives of study, and such concessions to the interests of the taught will almost certainly enhance learning.

We suggest that the whole imbroglio caused by the learning outcomes fad stems chiefly from two errors (Hussey and Smith 2002). The first has already been pointed out: statements about the *quality* and *extent* of knowledge, understanding, critical analysis, skilled behaviour and so on, are always relative to an educational context. What such statements *mean* is always relative to the level and nature of the course of study. It depends on what is judged to be appropriate at that level and in relation to the kind of course it is. A course on rock forming minerals in the first year of a geology degree will be quite different from such a course in the third year, and both would be quite different from a course with that title as only a minor part of a degree in palaeontology.

However, if the meaning of 'learning outcomes' depends on what is judged to be appropriate at a given level, this brings us directly to the second, more subtle error. The fad for precisely worded learning outcomes rests on a misunderstanding of knowledge. Philosophers have distinguished between different kinds of knowledge, two of which concern us here. Gilbert Ryle (1949) distinguished between 'knowledge that' and 'knowledge how'. The latter is now often called 'procedural knowledge' but Ryle's term seems more apposite. Roughly, 'knowledge that' is knowledge of facts: true statements such as 'frogs are amphibians', 'Charles Dickens wrote *Great Expectations*', 'all proteins contain nitrogen' and so forth. 'Knowledge how' refers to the possession of learned skills and abilities, such as being able to tap-dance, ride a bicycle, speak English, solve crosswords or keep discipline in a classroom. Unlike 'knowledge that', 'knowledge how' is not expressed in declarative sentences which are either true or false, it is generally demonstrated in performances.

The relationship between these two kinds of knowledge is a complicated matter, but we need only focus on one aspect: whether 'knowledge how' can be expressed in terms of 'knowledge that'. That is, whether you can express a skill or learned ability in a set of true propositions. In some cases this seems possible. If a person is able to access their emails on a computer they can (so long as they are not a computer buff) generally put into words how they do so. Similarly, it is possible to describe in a more-or-less understandable way, how to prune rose bushes, wire up a three-point plug, spell 'necessary' or start a lawn mower. However, for anything more complicated the task of translation from 'knowledge how' to 'knowledge that' is much more difficult. Imagine trying to describe how to swim the breast-stroke, write a poem, tie up a shoelace, carve letters on a gravestone, parallel-park a car, dance a tango or tell a joke. The result in each case would be a very long and complicated piece of prose and, what is more, it would be quite useless as a means of teaching the knowledge to someone else. Try teaching someone to shape a cabriole leg purely by spoken instructions. Finally, there are almost certainly many everyday skills which cannot, whether in practice or in principle, be translated into 'knowledge that'. If psycholinguists are right, no one can explain all the rules of English grammar despite the fact that English speakers use them constantly. Similarly, it is almost certainly impossible to put into words how we compose music, find mathematical proofs, judge the motives or personality of others, and so on.

The point of this brief tour of a part of epistemology is that learning outcomes are, for the most part, an attempt to express 'knowledge how' in terms of 'knowledge that'. Consequently it is largely futile. Of course teachers and academics possess some 'knowledge that'. They can recite facts, describe things in declarative sentences and correct the statements of their students. However, most of the knowledge they possess is in the form of 'knowledge how'. The ability to judge the level at which to pitch a lecture; to identify just what it is that a student finds difficult; to spot that a concept is not understood; to recognise that a student's response is at the appropriate level; to detect that a seminar group is wandering off the subject, are all skills. They are skills learnt while passing through the educational system, from study, from watching others and so on.

Almost all learning outcomes are an attempt to express 'knowledge how' in a set of statements – 'knowledge that'. For example, to state that a student will critically analyse the impact of the World Bank on the problems of Nigeria, or understand the distinction between jealousy and envy, or describe the role of paternalism in *King Lear* is to try to put in words what, in the event, has to be judged by an experienced tutor. Only that tutor's '*knowledge how*' to evaluate critical analysis, understanding and description, at the relevant level, will determine how well the students have performed. Even the list of topics that it is appropriate to cover in a course stems from a general feel for the discipline concerned. The list reflects what is generally done in courses of the kind.

Perhaps a rationale could be given but that will only be a vague attempt to put into words what is generally practised by those in the profession.

If, as we have argued, the fad for trying to express learning outcomes in a precise language of "descriptors" is a futile exercise, this may explain why so many academics have complied so reluctantly with their use. Those who have embraced them enthusiastically and accepted them as precise statements, have done so, we suggest, because they have either wittingly or unwittingly interpreted them in the light of their expertise. It also explains why teachers and academics have found it so difficult to put into words how they do their job of teaching and assessing. This is not because they are too idle or too arrogant; nor is it because teaching is some mysterious, ineffable gift of genius. It is because it is an elaborate collection of skills which can be demonstrated in practice and recognised and criticised by others, including those upon whom they are practised. The skills, like most skills, can be shown but not usefully described.

In this chapter we have tried to illustrate the damaging effects of distorting educational practice by following a fad, the main motive for which is not educational excellence, but managerial convenience. In the next chapter we underline this message by showing how education can be enhanced by sensible and appropriate teaching and learning practices, including the proper use of such devices as learning outcomes.

8

The Other Side of Learning

In the previous chapter we presented a critique of the concept of learning outcomes as they have been interpreted. However, let us be clear, we are not condemning the idea of identifying sets of intentions, or advocating a free-for-all in which the outcomes of education are entirely arbitrary and unplanned; rather we are suggesting that in their current form learning outcomes are too narrowly conceived to provide a useful guide to both learners and teachers. In this sense the inflexible and unyielding pre-specification of intended learning outcomes is both reductive and ultimately damaging to learning. It is reductive in the sense that it condenses intentions down to what may be pre-specified, and antithetical to the processes of learning in so far as it is predominantly concerned only with narrow cognitive operations. The vision it holds out is the chilling one in which:

> a uniformed army of young adolescents all marching to the same drummer, towards the same objective, may be one that gladdens the hearts of technocrats, but it is a vision that has little or nothing to do with those delicious outcomes that constitute the surprises of educational experience.
>
> (Eisner 2000: 344)

Sir Ken Robinson (2006) laments the emphasis on cognitive operations, observing that: 'western education is concerned with the waist upwards, focusing on the head and slightly to one side.'

Had we but learned from the history of the Rational Curriculum Planning by Behavioural Objectives (RCPBO) movement in the United States and similar attempts in the United Kingdom in the 1960s and 1970s, we would not have embarked on the process of repeating history; indeed, as Marx noted, when history repeats itself there is humour to be found in the whole sad process. Certainly some of the excesses of the learning outcomes regime led to rubrics which are risibly misplaced: a blanket ban against the use of the verb 'under-stand'; the stricture that Level One Outcomes should not include the verb 'analyse'; its converse that 'understanding' or 'comprehension' has no place at Level Three and certainly not in postgraduate studies, or that statements of intended outcomes should not include reference to critical reflection until Level Three since it is well known that students are incapable of the process prior to that. All of which makes for sorry reading and even sorrier and misguided practice; as we suggest above, were it not so destructive, it would be laughable.

Beyond the obvious inanities and shortcomings of this approach to the specification of learning outcomes, lies a more fundamental misconception concerned with the processes of learning and development. The process implied by the Learning Outcomes movement is essentially linear, moving from the simple to the complex; a series of steps to be achieved moving onwards and upwards. It is not hard to trace the origins and development of this approach from the work of Bloom, Engelhart, Furst, Hill and Krathwohl's (1956) taxonomic hierarchies, or more recently Biggs's (1999: 47) approach advocating the notion of alignment and the use of a 'hierarchy of verbs that may be used to form curriculum objectives'. In advocating the notion of constructive alignment Biggs even goes so far as to state that in conditions of alignment,

> The students are 'entrapped' in this web of consistency, optimising the likelihood that they will engage the appropriate learning activities, but which paradoxically free students to conceal their own learning.
>
> (Biggs 1999: 26)

Having re-read the final part of this sentence, and indeed the entire paragraph and chapter of which it is a part, we remain mystified as to the emancipatory nature of the approach. In the cases of both Bloom et al. and Biggs, whether or not the intention was to represent learning and development as a unilinear process, the outcome has been that their statements have been interpreted as strict prescriptions, by both academics and administrators.

The notion of education as a linear process has evident attractions on the surface, but it is not the only explanation. Less evidently attractive and accessible are Jerome Bruner's ideas concerning education and development as cyclical processes in which, throughout their lives, individuals encounter the same fundamental and structuring concepts within disciplines at ever more complex levels in an ascending spiral requiring greater precision, more discriminate comprehension and increasing sophistication. For Bruner grasping the structure of a subject involves developing an understanding that enables other ideas to be related to it in significant ways. He claims that:

to be in command of these basic ideas, to use them effectively, requires a continual deepening of one's understanding of them that comes from learning to use them in progressively more complex forms.

(Bruner 1960: 13)

There may be problems with Bruner's ideas but we suggest that they do offer a view of learning that accords more closely with what teachers experience, whilst freeing them from the unilinear conception that prohibits the use of particular verbs and prescribes the use of others. The idea that development involves the progressive revisiting and revising of understandings, concepts and processes, remains one which accords more readily with classroom experience and practice.

8.1 Fuzzy Arenas

Classrooms are rarely tidy places, characterised as they are by a complex of agendas, activities and interactions. They represent arenas in which teachers seek to manage a confusing range of needs. Idiosyncratic motivations abound and teachers are required to fulfil, often at the same time, the roles of instructor, assessor, arbiter, and adviser, seeking to reconcile the needs of the students, the requirements of the programme and the constraints imposed by timetabling and facilities operating at full stretch. In Lampert's (1985) terms, teachers operate within conditions of 'constructive ambiguity'.

The potential for the unanticipated and the developmental is ever present. In the midst of that vortex of activities which exists in classrooms, it is a bold teacher who is prepared to seize those opportunities presented in order to consolidate and further the understandings of students. The attractions of remaining 'on script' focusing on those outcomes identified in the module outline are enticing, offering as they do, the semblance of certainty in an uncertain world. However, even the most risk averse teacher must be aware of opportunities arising which s/he might capitalise upon had s/he the courage to move 'off script' – away from the PowerPoint slides and neatly prepared handouts. In short, the appearance of a 'learning moment' or 'flashpoint' (Forest 1997) offers opportunities to consolidate existing learning, to reveal fresh, exciting and unexplored aspects of a subject, but also the possibilities of losing direction, focus and control. Such 'learning moments' or 'teaching moments' are familiar to all classroom practitioners: something occurs, a question, an observation – seeming a barely related contribution – which brings about a moment in which an opportunity can be seized, or rejected. To disregard, or ignore that moment, would be to lose the class, in more ways than one.

It was consideration of these kinds of opportunities which we encountered that first caused us to question the limitations of learning outcomes as they were presented in documentation. In framing learning outcomes for a foundation philosophy module, one of the authors had unwisely suggested that, as a result of participating in the module, students might 'enjoy' using philosophical ideas and methods. Enjoyment, he was informed, was neither something that could be measured, nor was it what philosophy was about. Goodnight Socrates. Motivating reluctant students is one of the first tasks of a teacher.

The dilemma for the teacher in all these situations is the extent to which they retain focus on the intended learning outcomes and the need to cover the content, and the need to grasp a valuable teaching opportunity. In relation to these kinds of issues we were attracted to the work of McAlpine and her colleagues (1999) which developed the notion of teachers' 'corridors of tolerance'. As teachers, each of us possesses a corridor of tolerance, an envelope within which responses from students fall or fail to fall. It represents the extent to which a cue is found to be acceptable or not. If a cue is acceptable then changes to teaching actions, in terms of either content or methods, will be made. If a cue is unacceptable the teacher draws on his/her experience to decide what, if any, actions to take.

Experienced teachers pay considerable attention to feedback, both directly and indirectly in terms of observing reactions, picking up on comments and reading non-verbal messages, amongst other reactions. They use these clues to determine if and how to modify what they are doing, making adjustments, providing examples and amplifications, questioning to ensure understanding, or possibly making more radical changes in relation to content and methods. Interestingly, McAlpine et al. provide evidence to demonstrate that teachers make these changes, not necessarily because they perceive that something is going awry, but occasionally because they think they can perceive an alternative which appears to offer a means of more effectively planting the learning into the students' lives, their experiences and understandings.

Clearly, what McAlpine et al. are describing involves teachers monitoring concurrently an extensive range of cues, and equally clearly, the room for misinterpretation must be considerable. If these processes are occurring in the consciousness of the teachers and the students are, at the same time, attempting to grapple with the complexities and unfamiliarities of what is being presented, then to describe classrooms as untidy, fuzzy is something of an understatement. Not to acknowledge this state of affairs would appear to be folly.

To summarise, experience suggests that, by and large, facilitating learning and understanding is not a mere matter of transference, but rather of creating the conditions which enable learners to construct and apprehend understandings through individual and group activities and processes. At the same time there is an emerging body of research evidence that appears to suggest complex and interactive processes are at work in classrooms as teachers seek to bring about learning in their students. It was upon these sorts of premonitions, observations and part understandings that we developed our thinking in relation to learning outcomes (Hussey and Smith 2002; 2003; 2008). Just as there are intended learning outcomes, so too are there emergent learning outcomes and just as some outcomes are predictable and desirable, it follows that some will be unpredictable and undesirable.

8.2 Emergent Learning Outcomes

Intended learning outcomes are those which are formulated and directed by the teacher or others and refer to what students should be able to demonstrate in terms of knowledge, skills and/or attitudes as a result of a learning episode. In contrast, emergent learning outcomes, as their title suggests, emerge from what happens in classrooms between learners, teachers and the curriculum. They cannot be entirely pre-specified, though some are more likely to occur than others and some may be more desirable than others (Hussey and Smith 2003).

In order to explore the relationship between intended and emergent learning outcomes, we proposed the following model.

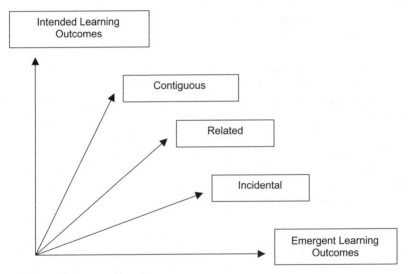

Figure 8.1 The range of learning outcomes.

Source: Hussey and Smith 2003. Reprinted by permission of the publisher (Taylor & Francis Ltd, http://www.tandf.co.uk/journals).

Contiguous Outcomes are sufficiently close to the intended learning outcomes to represent little more than a minor adjustment on the part of a teacher and would most probably take the form of presenting an example or an illustration of a principle or concept in order to clarify, or effect a link in the minds of the students, thereby supporting the intended learning outcomes for that teaching episode.

Related Outcomes represent more of a challenge to the teacher as the emerging topic, question or issue might not relate to the intended learning outcomes for the particular class, but could be seen to contribute to the overall consolidation of knowledge in that particular field of study. The question for the teacher here is whether or not they feel that the issue is worth pursuing at this time, or whether it should be shelved for subsequent consideration. Dilemmas presented might well be resolved by a response such as 'That's a really interesting issue you have raised there and it's one that we will be focusing on in Week X when we look at Y. So, in the meantime can you keep it in mind? We'll come back to it.'

Incidental Outcomes often take the form of more general issues and questions about the overall topic and/or relate to students' approaches to study and learning. In a sense the decision for the teacher is more clear-cut here, since the issues and queries raised often refer, not to the topic under enquiry, but to broader aspects such as, 'How does the study of X relate to the study of Y?' – questions which the teacher might well feel fall outside his/her remit, or which require individual follow-up with that student.

We mentioned previously notions of desirability and predictability in relation to learning outcomes, both intended and emergent. Clearly, as teachers, we have clusters of intentions when we are working with groups of students, intentions which we would like to address and achieve, and others which we might be prepared to tolerate. With experience we can, with a fair degree of accuracy, predict what issues might arise, where students are likely to encounter difficulty and what we consider to be desirable outcomes. However, whilst we might be able to predict that a particular set of concepts might represent something of a bear trap to students, occasionally we can be rocked back on our heels by an unexpected question, reaction or interpretation. At these moments whilst the teacher searches to try and understand and give reason to this apparently unique or unusual response, the teacher also has to make a judgement about the desirability of the direction in which the response is likely to take things. It might be that issues of an inappropriate ethical or legal nature will be raised. Figure 8.2 sets out the decision alternatives.

Quadrant A is largely unproblematic in presenting the desirable and predicted and, as such, represents the achievement of an intended learning outcome.

In **Quadrant B** the teacher is faced with an unanticipated situation, but it is one which contributes to the achievement of the intended learning outcomes and therefore presents an opportunity, possibly in the form of a 'learning moment' for the teacher to capitalise upon.

By contrast **Quadrant C** represents an outcome which the teacher is able to predict with some degree of accuracy, yet it is one which is undesirable or

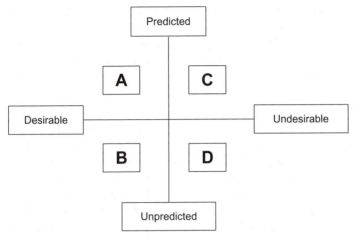

Figure 8.2 A model for learning outcomes.

Source: Hussey and Smith 2003. Reprinted by permission of the publisher (Taylor & Francis Ltd, http://www.tandf.co.uk/journals).

potentially disruptive to student learning. Outcomes here commonly take the form of common bear pits into which the unwary learner can fall and which can set back learning. The dilemma for the teacher in this situation concerns whether s/he steers students around this difficulty in order to consolidate current learning, subsequently to return to this difficult area, or whether student learning might best be served by allowing them to blunder into the trap and then have to work their way out of it.

Quadrant D represents a potentially dangerous and dysfunctional outcome. It is both undesirable and unpredicted, taking all parties by surprise. Whilst each participant will have their own views about notions of desirability, it is up to the teacher to make a judgement in these circumstances.

Far from being convenient and well defined repositories of intentions, learning outcomes then comprise much more complex clusters of intentions, perceptions and agendas. Whilst seeking to work with students to achieve a short and relatively loosely associated set of intentions, both teacher and students must negotiate a confusing, ambiguous and uncertain course in which they might encounter challenging surprises, even the 'delicious' outcomes of Eisner (2000), each and all of which require decisions to be made in a rapidly shifting context; or that 'swiftly flowing river' of Lewis and Tsuchida (1998). As a consequence the framing of learning outcomes needs to be undertaken with some regard to the highly problematic nature of those activities which comprise learning and teaching.

The activities of teaching and learning being seemingly irreducible to precise definition in scientific terms, it follows that considerable reliance is placed on metaphors. Our thinking owes much to the early work of Fox (1983) who draws attention to the ways in which different metaphors of teaching give rise to different vocabularies; in the transfer metaphor the teacher instructs and directs the student whilst the travelling metaphor refers to the notions of guiding and accompanying. It is here that we reach the crux of the matter with regard to learning outcomes.

Learning outcomes could be said to be at the "pointy" end of things, they represent what happens in those transactions between students, teachers and the curriculum. They represent the summation of ideas, assumptions and opinions concerning the nature and purposes of education. The way that they are expressed, the metaphors which are implied by their expression in behavioural and "point-at-able" terms, reflect the discourse to which they belong. Too often, as we have illustrated in the previous chapter, learning outcomes are expressed in reductionist terms, they fragment and separate, their governing assumption being that if actions such as understandings or the performance of a skill can be reduced to constituent parts, then upon successful achievement of all those elements, the whole can be put together and expressed as understanding or performance.

In contrast to this view we favour a more liberal and emancipatory discourse, one in which emergent learning outcomes can be accommodated and utilised in order to promote and consolidate learning. As the reductionist discourse seeks closure and convergence, so the liberal discourse seeks openness and divergence. Given that one of the central purposes of higher education is to produce autonomous individuals capable of operating successfully in a range of different circumstances and well able to live with rapidly changing contexts, it follows that the undergraduate career must represent a process of transition in which the student moves from an initial position of relative dependence upon the teacher to one of increasing independence from the teacher, and interdependence with others. Such a transition has profound implications for curricular and pedagogic arrangements that we will be returning to. However, what we are suggesting at this point is that in order to support and facilitate such a transition, learning outcomes will need to reflect the stage of development that the student has reached and will need to be framed by both teachers and students in order to accommodate their increasing independence.

Sadly, the current context of higher education, with its disproportionate emphasis on pre-specified outcomes and targets, represents one of the principal obstacles to achieving such an evidently practical and functional end. The language of the machine, or of the master and followers, exerts a strong influence; we continue to "roll out" new solutions, we seek to "drive" or "ratchet" up standards, students' progress is "tracked", particular concerns and issues are "targeted" whilst performances are compared against benchmarks. Within the implied metaphors the developing student is either a member of a flock, driven hither and yon at the whim of a master (and it usually is a master), or worse still, just some inanimate object on a conveyor belt – the image of a remorseless production line arises. Pink Floyd's lyric, 'It's all right, we told you what to dream' or their 'Wall' lyrics, seemingly so banal at the time they first appeared, take on a much more profoundly chilling aspect. However, the images conjured and the vocabularies employed retain a seductive appeal to the managerial mind. As Malcolm and Zukas (2001: 35) put it:

> the language of objectives, outcomes, competences and empowerment of the learner has 'seduced' both policy makers and practitioners in many areas of education.

This quotation raises a disturbing irony which is that these approaches and the language in which they are couched refer to an emancipatory discourse of empowerment, whilst advocating a structured approach which is entirely at odds with freedom. At the same time they offer the illusion of comforts and certainties of control.

In contrast to the reductionist ideology of intended learning outcomes, the genuinely emancipatory and developmental approach we wish to supplant it with, appears weak and tenuous. To speak of emancipation currently is to invite scorn and suggestions of a return to the "failed" and discredited ventures of the past – consider, for example, the connotation with which notions of "progressive education" are freighted. Not only is the vocabulary of emergent learning outcomes and associated practices perceived as redolent of previous failures, but perhaps, most significantly, they appear to open the doors to uncertainty and the nightmare visions of the loss of control: the door to the secret garden might not only have been opened, but ripped from its hinges.

We do not claim that this is an original view, being gratified to read the work of Knight (2001) urging us to break away from the discourses of learning outcomes, and Parker (2003) calling for a reconceptualising of the curriculum. More recently the TLRP (2005) has drawn attention to the restrictive and linear consequences of notions of alignment.

Naïve though it may seem, however, we are suggesting that it is only by developing such a broader, liberal and more generous conception of the purposes of higher education in general, and the role of learning outcomes in particular – one which engages not only the cognitive, but the social, interpersonal and affective domains, but which is also expressed at classroom level in the accommodation of both intended and emergent learning outcomes – that we will begin to enable the system to promote and produce empowered, autonomous and truly adaptable individuals who will be our best bet for survival in times of increasing turbulence and change.

Mention of our times of increasing turbulence and change suggests that, before we continue with our task of making positive suggestions for reform, we should lift our eyes from the furrows and look at the hills. We need to take a broader view of our topic and establish what we think universities ought to be and what problems they face in our time. These will be the subjects of our next chapter.

9
A Broader View

Observant readers will have noticed that there has been a change of tone in the book. The first seven chapters contained an examination of what is offered as higher education in many of the United Kingdom's universities and they were intended to be critical, while Chapter 8 began the task of making some positive suggestions. Before we continue with constructive proposals for reform it is necessary to step back and take a broader view. We need to say what we think a university ought to be, why we think universities are valuable and what challenges they face in today's world. These reflections will then inform the remaining chapters, which will develop our ideas for changing things for the better.

There is an obvious problem: these topics are enormous. The issues involved are worthy of, at least, a whole book. Indeed, many books have been written about the nature of a university; their forms and functions; their values and purposes, and the problems they face today. Since the nineteenth century divine, John Henry Newman, delivered lectures published under the title *The Idea of a University* in 1852, there has been an abundance of books and articles on similar themes, many with a similar title (Newman 1976). We cannot hope to match the detail and subtlety of this huge literature and will not try to do so. What follows is a sketch, over-simplified and crude, and much of it fairly unsurprising, but, we hope, sufficient for its purpose. It will not be an extensive or profound analysis, but will merely serve to point out the path we are taking in this book and explain why we trudge in that direction and not others.

We will begin, in Section 9.1, by saying in broad terms why we think we need universities and what functions they should fulfil. These functions are stated boldly and simply so as to offer a standard or ideal against which we can test possible models of higher education. In Section 9.2 we will sketch the major factors which impinge upon a society, such as the UK, when it attempts to construct and maintain a tertiary educational system. In Section 9.3 we undertake a critical examination of three possible scenarios of the future shape of higher education in the UK, bringing out the merits and demerits of each. Which of these scenarios corresponds most closely to the kind of system we will eventually get depends on the factors identified in Section 9.2 but, most particularly, government education policy. Section 9.4 is a brief discussion of rather more esoteric cultural and intellectual forces which may impinge on our educational system. Our conclusions are presented in Section 9.5, where we offer our ideal university system.

9.1 Why We Need Universities

We value universities primarily because of the functions they serve, and these functions are related to what we take to be worthwhile and desirable. There is not unanimity in these matters between the various interested parties – the general population, students, politicians, employers, academics, educational theorists and so on – but we will present what we consider to be a credible account and defend it as best we can. The functions and the values they reflect can be arranged in a rough hierarchy, beginning with the most important. This too is a matter of dispute and we will discuss objections throughout the chapter, after stating the functions boldly.

1. **Individual flourishing** Universities are a means by which individuals can flourish and find fulfilment. Both the students passing through and the academics working within the institutions are enabled to develop their talents, skills and capacities in ways, and to an extent, that would be very difficult if not impossible without a university. The processes by which this is achieved are, of course, learning, teaching, research and scholarship, together with a kind of communal life that is very difficult to define but of great importance: a living together and a sharing of ideas and experiences often beyond the boundaries of individual disciplines. The cultural life of a university – its clubs and associations as well as its informal networks and activities – is of immense importance in shaping the education produced.

   This function of a university is both of intrinsic and utilitarian value: it enables people to flourish and it equips them to find rewarding employment and a fulfilling life. As R. S. Peters (1967) argued, if someone is educated they are altered for the better; they have acquired something thought to be worthwhile; something that is not inert but which transforms their life.

2. **Social flourishing** Universities enable societies to flourish and prosper. They are a means – not the only means but a vital one – by which cultures develop, economies grow, wealth is created and societies change. They contribute to the quality and quantity of life, even for those who do not have university educations. Universities

contribute to the task of enabling societies to prosper and to hold their own in a competitive world, but above all, they contribute to the aura and calibre of a society.

3. **Preservation of freedoms**   Universities act, or should act, to preserve and exercise freedom of thought and expression. They are, or ought to be, centres of analysis and critical evaluation of society and international affairs. In this way they can contribute to the quality of our lives and protect us against abuses of power and influence. They can watch and criticise cultural, social and political changes and, by doing so, help to maintain or change our political system, protect our rights and clarify our responsibilities. They can offer independent judgements upon the activities of leaders at home and abroad, and can examine and critique governments and societies around the world. This critical role also extends to the arts and literature, morality and religion. It is for these reasons that the plea for academic freedom is not a selfish plea.

4. **Creativity**   Universities are a source of innovation and invention; centres for research and development, and generators of ideas. They have this function in science, technology, the arts, politics, management and religion: indeed all areas of our lives. If we value a lively, vigorous culture, progress in medicine, improving social services, better food production, improved leisure industries, and a dynamic, productive and competitive economy, we need the contribution of an active university sector.

   One important aspect of this function is the role of universities in undertaking "fundamental" research – that is research into matters underlying a whole area of knowledge and generally remote from commercial, social or military exploitation; and "pure" research – research done for its own sake or motivated simply by curiosity rather than for some extrinsic purpose such as its potential commercial or military value. Although knowledge is often valued for its utility, it can also be valued for its own sake, and this is particularly true within the arts and humanities. It is certainly the case that universities have traditionally pursued research in areas neglected by those outside.

5. **Repositories of knowledge**   Universities are reservoirs of knowledge, understanding and skills. They help to preserve and interpret our cultural heritage. They are places where individuals and teams can exercise scholarship and hone their skills. Some of the knowledge is lodged in the minds of those working in the universities while some is contained in the libraries, data bases and museums they possess.

6. **Dissemination of knowledge**   Universities function so as to

disseminate knowledge, skills and expertise. They are centres of knowledge transfer in science, technology, the arts and the humanities, and of influence in matters of political, moral and aesthetic values. Obviously the activities of teaching and learning are an essential part of life internal to the university, but it characteristically extends into the wider community. Dissemination is achieved not only through the production of students, but via publications, consultancies, exhibitions, conferences, "think tanks", government advisers, public lectures, media representation, direct involvement in industry and so on.

It is a vital feature of this process of dissemination that the knowledge involved is as unbiased and untainted by ideological or commercial interests as possible. Where different perspectives and ideologies exist, this diversity should be available within the universities. Universities form a vital component of the "community of letters" and the "community of practice" within the professions. In many cases, writers, artists and indeed anyone who has an interest in, or need for, information can access it within a university. At a more mundane level, a "university town" generally has a special quality and the presence of students in a town can transform its local culture – sometimes even for the better.

7. **Gatekeeper to the professions**   Universities function as the "gatekeepers" for several of the professions. They have traditionally provided the training and hence the qualifications necessary for entry into law and medicine, and other professions such as nursing, management, architecture, engineering and teaching have followed, or are following, the same path. This role is valuable both because it helps to ensure standards within the profession and, more importantly, because it offers some protection to the public who are clients of the professionals.

9.2 Some Important Factors

Although they are not free from controversy, the functions listed above are widely seen as being of great value. Societies that are, or aspire to be, prosperous, liberal, democratic states generally embrace this model of higher education or something similar. Indeed it is difficult to see how such a society could emerge and survive in a competitive world without institutions serving the purposes described. However, there are formidable problems in creating, maintaining and improving such a system. In discussing them we have to take into account a number of important factors which will have fundamental effects upon the future of our universities. Unfortunately many of them are extremely difficult to predict and none can be forecast with precision. The recent economic crisis has already brought about unexpected changes.

Clearly, the future evolution of our economy is one such factor: we can only assume that we will remain a reasonably prosperous nation that can, one way or another, afford a higher education system not too unlike the one we have. Experience tells us that economic slow-downs and even recessions occasionally occur, but here we will not consider the possibility of a catastrophic decline. If climate change, major conflicts, huge challenges from overseas competitors, or the collective greed and incompetence of those in charge of commerce or politics, bring massive changes in our ability to sustain our university sector, then radically different circumstance would require a radically different book. However, there are other major factors which are much more likely to make profound differences in the medium and long term, and which we must consider. One is the policies adopted by future governments, another is the possibility of large demographic changes and another is the possibility of substantial cultural change. Obviously these factors are interrelated.

The picture we have sketched of government policies since the 1960s is that they set out with the intention of expanding higher education while preserving essentially the existing system. The difficulties, and especially the cost, of doing so led to the development of a greater variety of institutions than originally envisaged. To a few élite universities, now largely preserved in the Russell Group, were added numerous "red brick" institutions, some of which were would-be-simulacra while others tried to establish new forms. To these were added ex-polytechnics and colleges of higher education which had their roots in a different tradition: they had their managerial structures and internal organisations already established and simply tried to adapt them to their new status. Some universities have adopted measures designed to cope with the demands of mass education, such as modular degrees or virtual learning systems; others have just built bigger lecture theatres and seminar rooms large enough to contain a mass audience, while some have tried to cling on to their traditional tutorial systems. The result is a stratified sector consisting of disparate forms all pretending to be the same kind of entity.

Future governments have choices to make. They may persist in trying to give an increasing number of students a "traditional" university experience, or they may give up the pretence and deliberately choose a tiered system with several kinds of institution serving very different purposes. They may persist with a largely publicly funded sector or follow the recent trend in the rest of our economy and favour private provision; or they may push the existing system towards ever greater collaboration with employers in the commercial and industrial sectors, in the hope that they will shoulder much of the burden.

The formidable cost of higher education and the difficulty of raising taxation to pay for it have already led to radical changes, such as the ending of free student grants, the introduction of tuition fees and the, less visible, chronic under-funding. In other areas of the economy, privatisation and private-public partnerships have been very popular with governments of all political shades – for today they are only shades of the same colour – and this may point the way in education. Similarly, a market system with a strong emphasis on competition may be seen as a way of producing "efficient" education and a reduction in costs. Devolution of governmental powers to Scotland, Wales and Northern Ireland has already produced important divergence within the UK tertiary sector and this is likely to increase. It will have the benefit of providing us with a valuable means of comparing different policy choices – social experimentation on a large scale.

Demographic changes are not entirely independent of government policies. The birth rate of the indigenous population dips and rises over time and makes significant, if predictable, changes to the student population, but it appears fairly immune to direct manipulation by governments. By contrast, inward migration is greatly affected by policy changes. Depending on the size and composition of the immigrant population, especially the age-profile, and on their cultural attitudes to education, so the future student population will change. In several European nations, including Britain, the native birth rate is hardly enough to sustain the present size of population so any increase, including in student numbers, is likely to come from immigration. Immigration also has an effect by being used to keep down wages in certain industries, so lowering the attractiveness of some courses of study. Thus, government policies could make a difference; for example, if unemployment rises sharply we are likely to see dramatic attempts to reduce immigration. Once again, predicting future policies, or their success, is almost impossible.

Government policies also influence the numbers of students coming from the different social classes. As already mentioned, the middle classes have been much more able than others to avail themselves of the opportunities provided by the massive increase in university student numbers. If future policies were to aim at encouraging participation by working class youngsters this might make a difference to overall numbers. Alternatively, governments could decide to shift a large tranche of young people into craft courses and various "applied" areas of study and take them out of the university sector altogether. The recent introduction of new diploma courses may be a step in this direction. It is obvious that these changes in the size of the student population are extraordinarily difficult to predict, yet they would have profound implications for universities.

Universities UK, the body that represents the executive heads of UK universities, commissioned a demographic study (Universities UK 2008a) which tries to project forward to 2019–20 and to 2026–27 to give some indication of the demand for higher education. The report recognises that there is a large margin of error accompanying such predictions, due to the uncertainties already mentioned. In brief, the report predicts that there will be a decline in the number of full-time undergraduate students between the base-line of

2005–06 and 2019–20 of about 5.9 per cent for the UK as a whole, varying from a drop of 13.2 per cent in Northern Ireland to 4.8 per cent in England. This is a serious matter. It represents a fall of over 70,000 students and may lead to mergers or even closures among the less attractive institutions. Just as their doors close the demand seems likely to rise, mainly due to immigrants and their children. By 2026–27 there is likely to be an increase, at least in England, giving an overall increase in the UK of 0.8 per cent from the 2005–06 base-line.

During the same period it is thought that the part-time student population, consisting mainly of older age groups, is likely show a modest growth. Here there is uncertainty due to recent government policy to withdraw funding for students who wish to study for a qualification at an equivalent or lower level than one they already possess. This may reduce undergraduate numbers, especially those choosing part-time courses, by around 40,000. What it will do for the widely espoused need for people to be flexible and switch careers to meet new demands, is debatable. If you have a master's degree in chemistry and want to move to a job in plumbing then, presumably, you must start with a doctorate.

Alongside these demographic changes there is the matter of overseas students. The UK higher education system has been very successful in attracting students from all over the world and they have made a vital contribution, not just to the cultural and intellectual richness of the sector, but also to its income. With a few special exceptions, foreign students pay higher fees – sometimes much higher fees – than the home-grown equivalents. However, the future flow of such students depends on several factors only some of which are in the control of UK governments. As Third World and developing countries build their own university systems so we may have more difficulty in attracting their young people to study here. Similarly, other countries are competing with us in this lucrative market, even conducting classes in English where necessary. As we have seen recently, our foreign policy decisions may also raise or lower our popularity in the world.

Perhaps the most important thing that attracts foreign students to Britain is the very high standard of our universities. At present British universities have an astoundingly high ranking amongst the world's higher education institutions. According to the Times Higher Education Supplement ranking, Britain has four universities, Cambridge, Oxford, Imperial College London and University College London, in the top ten, all the rest being American; and we have 18 in the top one hundred (Times Higher Education 2007). The table constructed by China's Shanghai Jiao Tong University includes only Oxford and Cambridge in the top ten (Ash 2008), but even this is remarkable for such a small country. Continued success in attracting overseas students depends on maintaining this high ranking, and it is evident that our lower-ranking universities benefit from the reflected glory. Nevertheless, even if our élite universities maintain something close to their present high status, if we embark on a starkly stratified system, foreign students may come to understand that a place in the lesser institutions is not worth the expense. As mentioned in Chapter 6, students at many UK universities do not get a very good bargain for their money. Alternatively, if our reputation is not harmed too much but our universities continue to be under-funded, they may be driven to recruit an ever higher proportion of foreign students just for the income it provides, and even to the exclusion of our own young people. Again, these eventualities are not easy to predict.

Cultural and other social changes may be difficult to identify but they also have an impact upon our universities. In the last half century we have seen a fairly rapid shift to a post-industrial society with a switch from workshop to office. The demand for skilled technically educated designers, engineers, chemists and such like has given way to a need for people in the service industries, entertainment and information technology. Several university science departments have closed despite the persisting, indeed vital, importance of science and technology in the world's economies.

The indifference shown by governments can also have an effect: for example the indifference shown to the gross inequalities in salaries and bonuses, especially the run-away rewards for those in higher management and in the financial sector, produced a drift from science, engineering and technology. Recent events may modify this but it seems that in industry, as much as in education, those who manage the primary activities are more able to extract rewards than those who carry out those primary activities. In addition, our traditional snobbery about crafts and skills will almost certainly remain and distort ambitions and rewards in those areas.

More subtle changes may be at work in attitudes towards science and learning in general. When universities recruited almost exclusively from the wealthy and middle classes for whom university was an expectation, popular culture and attitudes were of little importance, but now that they reach out much more widely, these factors may have more significance. The rise of individualism with its stress on choice and freedom may have contributed to the growth of the "new age" culture with its taste for the exotic and mystical, as opposed to the strictures and rigours of science and rationality. It seems plausible that popular culture, which we can caricature as having a taste for celebrity, sport, popular music, pseudo-science, alternative medicine, pop-psychology, alcohol, recreational drugs and the ineffectual rebelliousness of youth, may have an effect on decisions about going to university and upon the choice of university courses. It may, for example, be one of the factors producing the trend away from the natural sciences. But not only is popular culture mercurial, its effects may be exaggerated: even if the caricature given above is accurate, the fact is that its growth has been accompanied by an increase in the take-up of university places. It is even possible, although unlikely, that the UK will follow trends in the USA and see an increase in the popularity and political influence of fundamentalist religious faiths, which may eventually damage the sciences. The long term effects of our passion for faith-based schools are, as yet, a mere cloud as small as a man's hand. Francis Wheen's (2004) *How Mumbo-Jumbo Conquered the World* gives a satirical critique of this slide to un-reason.

While the fashion for homeopathy, creationism and other such silliness may be bewildering and frustrating, the real threat to science and rationality comes from more powerful forces: on the one hand the distorting power of big business and powerful commerce, and on the other the relativism of some intellectual movements (Hind 2008). We will discuss the dangers of universities becoming too close to business later. At a more intellectual level, the drift towards postmodernism in the arts and in philosophy, with its tendency to embrace a kind of permissive relativism and a denigration of "élitist" claims to truth and knowledge by "Western" science, may ultimately undermine our Enlightenment values and our respect for reason. This issue will be discussed further in Section 9.4.

It is not all gloom. In recent times more money has been invested in primary and secondary education in the UK, and not only are more young people taking A-level examinations, or the equivalent, but an ever higher proportion are achieving the best grades. Sadly, there is a danger that the emphasis on competition between schools and on league tables may induce teachers to encourage children to study those subjects in which it is easiest to obtain high grades, and avoid those the students may have preferred or which the nation needs. Such unintended consequences of policies may have a marked effect at the tertiary level.

In this section we have sketched what are, we believe, the most important factors which will impact upon UK universities in the medium and long term. To try to make progress towards a conclusion concerning the kind of university system we would like to see, we will now discuss a number of practical alternatives, basing our discussion on another report commissioned by Universities UK.

9.3 Possible Paths and Their Hazards

Very wisely, the report on the effects of government policies (Universities UK 2008b) does not attempt to predict the future. Instead it explores three possible scenarios which might materialise by 2027, depending on the demographic changes and government policy choices. It is worth looking at these realistic scenarios and their implications because they will help us to home in on our ideal model.

The first scenario which they entitle 'Slow adaptation to change' envisages an evolution in which universities continue much as at present as campus-based institutions, competing for students and adjusting to the demographic changes as they come, but with only a relatively small growth of e-learning and part-time study. Since public funding is likely to match student numbers, universities will go though a period of struggle when numbers fall and there may be closures or mergers, although there may also be an incentive towards co-operation. The struggle will encourage the exploration of new degree programmes and various recruiting initiatives, which might include the lowering of entry requirements and qualifications of a reduced standard. Subjects which are in low demand may be abandoned despite their importance. Universities may be "encouraged" to cater increasingly towards the needs of employers, which may lead to a reduction in the choice of courses. There may be a modest growth in non-public or commercial providers who seek to exploit certain niche "markets". This scenario may also lead to some loss of reputation of the UK system.

To these observations we can add that this scenario preserves some of the most valuable aspects of our system, including the seven functions listed in Section 9.1. Academic staff will continue to undertake both teaching and research with reasonable independence of outside pressures. The full-time attendance and largely face-to-face learning will conserve at least part of the human contact and traditional academic qualities of the student experience. The universities will retain enough independence to maintain their roles in protecting freedoms, offering a critique of society, providing a source of relatively independent advice and knowledge, and in qualifying people for the professions. It may be that these valuable functions will not be served by all universities but they will survive.

The 'Slow adaptation to change' scenario does something to ward off the slide towards a stratified tertiary sector in which some institutions specialise in mass teaching while others continue with research and offer an expensive education for an élite, but this danger remains a real possibility. Much will depend on what happens to the funding of students and the imposition of higher top-up fees. The Universities UK (2008b) report assumes that the government will allow universities to increase the fees they demand and, if this happens, it may have a profound effect on the divergence of strands within the system. The top universities will be able to charge much more than those struggling at the bottom and, despite bursaries and special grants, this will inevitably lead to a divergence among students, largely according to social class. There may also be an increase in shorter, intensive degree courses designed to attract cost-conscious students.

The second scenario, dubbed 'market-driven and competitive', envisages a situation in which there is a highly competitive market and "non-traditional providers" are encouraged to enter. These private organisations, from within the UK and from outside, will, it is suggested, cherry-pick the most lucrative areas and take over failing public institutions that wither in the heat of competition. The number of traditional universities or "multi-mission institutions" will be reduced and we will see a marked increase in specialist or niche providers. More private money will come into the system and there will be an expectation that increased competition will lower costs overall. This will lead to a reduced and much more targeted public expenditure, as public institutions lose business to the private providers. There will be more choice for students and more are expected to switch to part-time courses or e-learning. This, in turn, will put even more pressure on large, campus-based universities. It is suggested that some of the élite universities may try to leave the publicly funded sector and sell off their least profitable activities.

Given recent trends in government policies, this scenario – or something close to it – is very likely to materialise. The attraction of a private enterprise, market-driven system leading to reduced public expenditure will be difficult to resist, despite recent lessons from the banking sector. The report envisages some disadvantages: a substantial reduction in the reputation of UK universities, at home and overseas, and a decisive turn towards a stratified system in which a few universities pursue research and the rest are confined purely to teaching. The cost to students is likely to rise, as may those to employers. Academics will find themselves corralled into either the élite universities, mainly engaged in research, or into teaching institutions dealing with large numbers on fairly narrow courses tailored to niche markets.

We suggest that there are serious problems with this competitive market model, but it will be convenient to introduce the third and last scenario before we discuss them, because it raises similar issues. The University UK report (2008b) calls the third scenario 'employer-driven flexible learning'. This portrays a situation in which public funding is increasingly restricted and increasingly regulated so as to target specific needs: the process being guided by the demands of employers and students. The cost to the taxpayer will be significantly reduced while employers will pay considerably more. The scenario envisages a large scale switch to "part qualifications"; that is, certificates, diplomas and "foundation degrees" for narrowly defined areas of study and specific skills, with far fewer full-time courses for honours degrees. (Foundation degrees are typically two-year programmes in very restricted subject areas; a third year being required to transform it into an honours degree.) There would be much greater emphasis upon credit accumulation and transfers between courses and institutions. This would be achieved by massively increasing the proportion of part-time study and the use of e-learning, together with a transformation of the higher education sector. Tertiary education would be provided by a highly stratified range of institutions, including new private providers, "virtual" colleges and close co-operative alliances between universities and employers.

For the students there will be, the report suggests, lower costs, or fees no higher than today. The academic workforce will have to become much more flexible. Many will be self-employed, and many will move back and forth between the commercial and industrial and academic spheres. The chief difference between this scenario and the previous one, it is claimed, is greatly reduced competition within the system.

We suggest that there are serious dangers with both the 'market-driven and competitive' and the 'employer-driven flexible learning' scenarios. Both will involve a strong market ethos and, despite the claims of the report, both will involve competition. Even in the 'employer-driven' model, universities and private companies will vie with each other for lucrative contracts with the big companies. (What the invaluable small companies in emerging areas of technology will do we cannot say.) Private companies will cherry-pick the most profitable contracts. Whether academic standards will be maintained is debatable: markets are likely to attract the usual spivs and barrow boys, and are likely to drive down standards. Students will have more choice of means to study but few of the courses will provide anything approaching a traditional university degree. For the great majority of young people the aim will be to get a useful qualification rather than an education.

Even the choice may evaporate in times of economic recession: profit-based businesses do not have the endurance of publicly funded universities and employers will abandon training – for training, rather than education, is what it will be – in times of economic hardship. In any case, it may always be cheaper to import ready-trained workers from abroad. Employers may find that staff, who have been narrowly trained in specific areas, are rapidly out of date, even before their training is complete. Under both scenarios it is likely that there will be a move towards ever shorter, and ever cheaper, courses and two-year degrees and "foundation degrees" may become the norm outside the few élite institutions. Higher education will become more similar to the further education sector.

But, as the number of traditional universities decreases, the biggest dangers are to the values and functions which we listed at the start of this chapter. Both scenarios are likely to accelerate the drift towards a utilitarian view of education. Students will be increasingly encouraged to seek job-specific quali-fications; whether because of the cost, or because, in the 'employer-driven' model, there will be little else from which to choose. Opportunities for a rounded education will be restricted to the few – and those mainly selected from the privately educated. The nation will get a workforce trained in what-ever is most lucrative or whatever big business and multi-national companies think they need.

The changes envisaged by the 'market-driven and competitive' and the 'employer-driven flexible learning' scenarios raise the question of the relative value between the first and second of the functions of universities listed: that is between the importance of "individual flourishing" and "social flourishing". It could be argued that since the community pays for the uni-versities its benefits should come before those of the individual, especially as a prosperous and successful nation will be better for the individuals it contains. However, there are real dangers if the flourishing of individuals is subordinated to the interests of the state or the business world. Most universities and all other tertiary educational institutions may come to be seen as merely training facilities, designed to produce the workforce required by industry or state institutions. We might soon see a situation in which a fortunate few could choose a university education while the rest were herded through the system as industrial, commercial and social fodder.

Against this it may be argued that most people want an education or training – and they don't much care which – that will lead to rewarding employment, and society needs people with useful skills not education in esoteric, scholarly subjects that happen to have excited the interest of individuals. The trouble is that, in a system where a large proportion of the population have access to something like a traditional university, they have a genuine choice, but once the system is changed to one providing specific training courses, the choice of a well-rounded university education, that is a liberal education, will have disappeared – for most people. Another problem is that both governments and industry are not infallible in their predictions of what specific skills they will require. The benefits of a more general education might shine through when we have over-produced IT specialists and nurses but under-produced physicists and mathematicians – or the other way round. Of course, our present university system can and does produce specialists, but even they study within a rich environment, and the institutions have within themselves a flexibility that our two scenarios might lose, especially when there is heavy private financial commitment in producing a certain "product".

The effect on research of the 'market-driven and competitive' and the 'employer-driven flexible learning' scenarios is likely to be devastating. Only a few remaining prestigious universities will undertake it and they are likely to have to find funding from private sources. The effect on the humanities could be very serious indeed, for it is not obvious who will pay for the probings of historians, the critical enquiries of literature dons or the analytical investigations of philosophers. They are not such saleable goods as to be worth funding. As for a critique of governments, foreign policy, business and other aspects of our society, these could dwindle to nothing. In a market place there is little room for stalls selling sticks with which to beat the stall owners.

Those seeking an academic career out of a wish to study a chosen subject and contribute to its progress will have to aim at employment in the few remaining prestigious, multi-mission, research universities. Even those whose main interest is teaching are likely to find themselves working in highly managed teaching institutions focusing on whatever specific and narrow qualifications are the demand of the day.

In the UK, the further education sector has been "encouraged" to go down the root of market-oriented, competing colleges with strong professional management, in a manner not unlike a combination of the two scenarios under discussion here. The consequences may give us a hint of what may be to come in higher education. In further education, it is claimed, the teaching staff has lost most of what autonomy it had, as control has passed to managers who are concerned with reducing costs and increasing throughput (Mather, Worrall and Seifert 2009). Lecturers find that they must teach whatever is needed with little regard for their wishes or expertise. Their jobs have become deskilled and they have become almost interchangeable units of labour, to be set to work wherever someone is needed. Class sizes, working conditions, and even the subject they teach are outside the control of the teachers. There are even rumours that colleges delay letting students take their exams, so as to retain their fees. This is not the stuff of a real university.

In totalitarian states and theocracies the functions of preserving freedoms and ensuring the right to question authorities are generally curbed or eliminated, and even in democracies they are often a source of irritation for the powerful. The need to preserve these functions is obvious. Perhaps what is not so obvious is that they must be preserved in a wide range of universities, preferably all, not just the few. In Britain it is a feature of our society that its élites – especially its political élites – tend to pass through a very narrow selection of universities. If the critical role is restricted only to them, then those doing the criticising will be dangerously close to those who go on to exercise political, industrial and commercial power, or who hold sway in the cultural sphere. Such incest is dangerous.

It would also have serious consequences for the sciences. The money for fundamental and pure research might be increasingly difficult to come by, and there is a real risk that science would be severely damaged as research became much closer to business and industry. The difficulty of financing unprofitable research, ensuring unbiased enquiry and the publication of negative results, will be enormous. There is already widespread concern about the influence of powerful commercial concerns and multi-national companies on what research is done and what is published. Even now, only 20 per cent of all trials on cancer treatment are published and of those sponsored by industry this falls to 5.9 per cent, of which, unsurprisingly, 75 per cent were positive (Goldacre 2008). Stories abound of reluctance to develop medicines for widespread but unprofitable diseases in the Third World; the reluctance to develop new antibiotic drugs because of their relatively short commercial life; the suppression of indications of serious side-effects from new drugs; funding of dubious research by dubious arms manufacturers; the patenting of discoveries that clearly ought to be available to all, and so on. The experience of John Sulston, who was awarded the Nobel Prize for his work on the human genome project in competition with a private company, is salutary in this respect (Sulston and Ferry 2002). The switch to a private-enterprise tertiary education system or one dominated by employers can only multiply these stories.

The situation concerning scientific research in the UK is very likely to be exacerbated by the notorious short-termism and short-sighted greed of our investors. Anything approaching long-term research is unlikely to be financed by the City of London or British commercial companies. Experience in the areas of biology, including genetics and pharmaceuticals, must teach us that few investors are willing to wait while inestimably difficult research may or may not produce, say, a drug, which then has to go through a series of trials before it may or may not be a marketable product. We have enough trouble already in these areas without resting the whole burden of research on commercial shoulders that are too narrow and sloping to carry the load. It is difficult to foresee the long term effects of the recent shift in research funding towards such areas as sports science and media studies (Hefce 2009). Given the changes in the economic structure of the UK, this may be what is needed but, in the long run, we may regret this change of emphasis. Re-establishing research facilities in the natural sciences, once lost, is an expensive business.

The idea that universities are repositories of knowledge which they can disseminate to those who need it, could be transmuted into the reality of universities as supermarkets where those who can pay can buy whatever they want to consider "knowledge". In the present system, universities have to find money from a mixture of sources including large charitable organisations, governments and industry, and the researchers are spread widely over many institutions. What governments and charities will finance when universities are closely associated with specific employers, is a puzzle. If university research becomes concentrated in a few institutions, each competing for finance from private sources, then the integrity of their research will be in jeopardy. Meanwhile, the majority of academics, who might have contributed their ideas and enthusiasm to research, will be trapped in colleges, teaching whatever the market or the employers demand.

The last of the functions listed – universities as gatekeepers to the professions – may come into question if higher education becomes a competitive, largely commercial system or a service industry to employers. At present it is the distance between the universities and the professions who employ their students that makes the gatekeeper role credible. The public has some chance of being protected from charlatans and incompetent practitioners so long as the distance is maintained and the qualities of the would-be professionals are judged by experts not too closely associated with the employers. There is a danger in a system that is not far removed from in-house training. There is little doubt that protection will be involved, but it is likely to be of the profession rather than its clients.

There is a connection here with the so-called "Mickey Mouse" and vocational degrees. We are, as a society, used to the idea that doctors and lawyers must have a university education and, in more recent times, others such as nurses, teachers and social workers have joined the band. We might be snobbish towards the leisure, catering and media industries wanting guaranteed entry qualifications, but much the same arguments apply wherever the public may need protection and quality assurance. In any area, if there is a real need for independent qualifications, an independent educational system seems essential. Whether that education needs to be at university level must be judged in individual cases and the judgement should be based on the intellectual breadth and depth required not on the perceptions of upturned noses. It is also worth reflecting that the blossoming of "Mickey Mouse" degrees may be due as much to the intense competition for students amongst institutions run by target-driven managers as it is by any real demand from the corresponding industry.

9.4 Cultural and Intellectual Challenges

Before we try to resolve, or at least navigate between, these difficult issues and identify the ideal university system, we must face some other challenges, more abstract yet, some would argue, just as pressing. Here the superficiality forced upon us by the necessary brevity will be even more evident because the topics are profound.

It is obvious that features of the culture prevailing in a society will have a powerful effect upon the nature and function of its universities and, indeed, whether such things exist at all. The contrasts between our universities in mediaeval times and now, or between "Western" universities and those in the Islamic world, are evidence enough. (For a sketch of the latter contrast see Kamal (2007).) However, the aspects of a culture that work to mould the education it embraces are subtle, and they produce their effects more slowly than economic or political forces. We have already mentioned the influence of some irrational features of popular culture and the recent resurgence of fundamentalist religious groups. Here we want to consider some other candidates.

One recurring theme is that today things are so much more complicated and the rate of change so much greater than in the past, that there is little possibility that an institution such as a university could keep up with the turmoil and function effectively. The implication is that an ivory tower is too static to serve any useful purpose so that, at best, we will need to change our universities quite fundamentally. For example, this might be seen as an argument for turning the higher education system over to market-oriented private enterprise companies, which would be better equipped to keep up to speed. Perhaps it would be unkind to suggest that it is the ageing commentators who are slowing down rather than the world speeding up, but anecdotal evidence suggests that every generation has made a similar complaint. If all these complaints were correct we would, by now, be moving fast enough to contradict Einstein.

An objective assessment of this claim is hampered by the difficulty of quantifying rates of social change or degrees of cultural complexity, so that we may compare different times and places. For example, the internet has almost certainly increased the amount of information available to us to a bewildering extent but it has also made access to that information much easier, as anyone who has ploughed through library index cards or back copies of journals will affirm. In any case, when we consider that our universities have survived through the Black Death, the Renaissance, the Reformation and Counter Reformation, the emergence of science, the English Civil War, the Agrarian Revolution and enclosures, the Industrial Revolution and two world wars, our present convolutions seem more manageable. A university possessing intelligent and informed minds with the time and freedom to think, seems to be admirably well suited to manage the change and complexities of our world effectively, at least as well as, say, the City of London or the banking system.

Ronald Barnett (2000) has taken this argument further by suggesting that we have entered the age of "supercomplexity", and that this has profound implications for our universities. He explains supercomplexity as follows:

> In short, professional life is increasingly becoming a matter not just of handling overwhelming data and theories *within* a given frame of reference (a situation of complexity) but also a matter of handling multiple frames of understanding, of action and self-identity. The fundamental frameworks by which we might understand the world are multiplying and are often in conflict. Of the multiplication of frameworks, there shall be no end.
>
> (Barnett 2000: 6)

He later elaborates on this explanation:

> We are in a situation of supercomplexity when our very frameworks for making the world intelligible are in dispute. The resulting fragility that confronts us is not that our frameworks are dissolving as such; rather it is that for any one framework that appears to be promising, there are any number of rival frameworks which could contend against it and which could legitimately gain our allegiance. We do not know and *we cannot know* with any assuredness who we are. We approach, it seems, a situation of collective anomie. There are no secure holds in the world.
>
> (Barnett 2000: 75. Italics in the original)

From these startling claims he eventually reaches some radical and serious conclusions that would transform our universities fundamentally, so we must examine what he says.

You will have gathered from the quotations that the idea of a 'framework' is pretty important to his argument. Unfortunately it is not easy to discover precisely what Barnett thinks these are. They cannot be simply different world-views or sets of beliefs about the world and ourselves, because there is nothing new or surprising in those. Such different perspectives have always bubbled up and we are quite used to dealing with them. Some are shown to be equivalent to others, some are shown to be mistaken, others distorted or partial, some persist and make a lasting impact, others fly up like rockets on bonfire night, sparkle for a while and are never seen again, and so on. Much depends on what area of human thinking and activity we are talking about. For example, science has some very effective decision procedures for sorting the dross from the diamonds, theology less so, the arts have developed a richness of critical traditions and so on. So, Barnett must mean that not only are we faced with innumerable "frameworks" but that our methods for evaluating them have been destroyed or shown to be illusory.

This radical interpretation is supported by the drastic conclusion he reaches concerning the consequences for universities:

> Much of the metaphysical baggage of 'the university' has to be ditched. Talk of knowledge, truth, justice and even emancipation have to be abandoned as carriers of the university. They require so many conditions and provisos to give them any substance that they end up, at best, as lumbering vehicles. These would-be upholders of the faith can be set aside.
>
> (Barnett 2000: 168)

This is dramatic stuff! Not only does it undermine completely most of the functions of universities listed in 9.1, it appears to abandon swathes of what we most valued about the Enlightenment. Universities can hardly be repositories and disseminators of knowledge if knowledge does not exist, and seeking truth is pointless if truth is an illusion. Similarly, they will struggle to preserve freedoms if such moral notions as justice and emancipation have lost their meaning, and the ideas of individual or social flourishing become profoundly problematic. For what is to count as a worthwhile education or an enhanced life or a better society, if we have no standards by which to judge?

For Barnett the traditional universities are dead, and they have to rise again as centres for 'incessant turmoil' and 'continual pandemonium' and 'sites for the continual production of revolutionary ideas' (2000: 172). This sounds very jolly. The trouble is, ideas, revolutionary or otherwise, have never been in short supply. Even a glance round the world will reveal people who believe in elephant-headed gods, Loch Ness monsters, virgin births, string theory, poltergeists, the healing power of crystals, quantum gravity, Noah's ark, and that Donald Duck shot President Kennedy. Ideas are ten-a-penny. The real challenge has always been finding ways of deciding between them. Barnett has to convince us that our cherished assortment of decision procedures has been shown to be useless: he must embrace an extreme version of postmodern relativism. This is confirmed by such exuberant claims as:

> Amid supercomplexity, the university has the dual responsibility not only of compounding uncertainty but also of helping us live with the uncertainty; even to revel in it. This is the task in front of the university. In a world where everything is uncertain, there is no other task.
>
> (Barnett 2000: 172)

Thus it seems that the roots of the problems facing our universities lie deep in the rich compost of postmodernism. Postmodernism is not a single or neat philosophical doctrine; rather it is a deep mulch of attitudes and opinions on topics ranging from architecture to zoology. Even within philosophy those who discuss postmodernism do not appear to agree about its nature – and this is a reflection of the kind of sentiment it favours (Lyotard 1984; Giddens 1991; Jameson 1991; Smart 1993). Postmodernists are disillusioned with all ideas of progress, rationality and truth which typify the Enlightenment tradition. They are sceptical of certainties and favour living with fluidity, eclecticism, anxiety and change. They reject such 'grand narratives' as Marxism that claim to give broad and objective explanations of human experience: the claims to know or to understand are considered pretentious. Quite naturally this set of attitudes affects the way postmodernists express themselves. They eschew careful analysis and definition, clarity and precision, and prefer irony, parody and poetic eloquence. To someone used to analytic philosophy this can seem like philosophy by arm waving.

The consequence is that debating with postmodernism is akin to shadow boxing with the lights out: not only is it difficult to know where your opponent stands, but even whether he or she is there at all. However, perhaps it is possible to tease out one feature of postmodern philosophy with some confidence: its relativism. The 'perhaps' here indicates that there are some postmodern philosophers, such as Rorty (1991), who are patently relativists yet deny that they are (Haack 1993). A thing can be said to be 'relative' if statements about it are only intelligible when provided with a context. For example, an aardvark is heavy in comparison to a termite, but light in comparison to an elephant, so to call something 'heavy' or 'light' always requires a specific background. Relativism takes many forms (Harré and Krausz 1996; Haack 1998; Baghramian 2004). It can be argued that morality, aesthetics, truth, knowledge, conceptual schemes, or rationality are relative to individuals, cultures, communities, world views, languages, scientific paradigms and so on. The result is an imbroglio of arguments in the philosophical literature which we cannot hope to untangle here.

For example, a relativist may claim that truth is relative to an individual. This is 'subjectivism': the idea that what is true for me may not be true for you.

Notice that it is not enough to claim that what I *believe* to be true, you may *believe* to be false – that is a commonplace difference of opinion. Relativism involves the claim that the *same* proposition, such as 'Air contains carbon dioxide', can actually be true for one person but false for another. Consequently there can be no such things as 'objective' or 'universal' or 'absolute' truth: whether anything is true depends to which individual's perspective you are referring.

Alternatively, truth or knowledge can be said to be relative to a culture, to a community, to a conceptual scheme, to a language or to a scientific theory. Again we must be clear: of course some communities may count some things as knowledge which other communities do not, but that is not enough for relativism. The relativist must insist that these claims do not conflict, so both can be right – that is to say there is no independent, objective way of deciding which community is right, or if neither is. Conceptual relativism claims that it is possible to divide up, describe and categorise the world in an indefinite number of ways, many of which are incompatible with each other. Since there is no neutral or "God's eye view" by which we can choose between them, we cannot grant the privilege of superiority or correctness to any one of them. Even natural science is just one story among many and it is no more valid or accurate than the tales told by shamanists or mystics. The claim may be yet more drastic: that even rationality itself is relative to a culture or a language, so there is no universal logic or correct way of reasoning.

There can be no doubt about the seductiveness of various forms of relativism and, helped on by the rakish glamour of postmodernism, it has become a popular fashion amongst intellectuals, artists and the like. It has two very attractive features. It cocks a snook at the authorities – the scholars, scientists, mathematicians, logicians and assorted know-alls who claim to tell us what is right and good and true – and it allows us to be tolerant, open-minded and generous towards alternative ideas and cultures. It rules out such things as the cultural imperialism of "Western science" or the traditional canons of "good" literature and "great" art.

Unfortunately, relativism has some disadvantages that seem to be less visible to its adherents. If there is no objective truth then we cannot, for example, deny those who say that AIDS can be cured by having intercourse with a virgin, or contradict the Pakistani clerics who tell parents that a polio vaccine is an American plot to sterilise their children (Walsh 2007). Similarly, moral relativism of the form which claims that 'X is morally good' means no more than 'X is approved of by me' is wonderfully tolerant of the great variety of moral rules that people adopt, but it also leaves us unable to tell the child molester that he is morally wrong to do what he is doing. We can stop him by force but we are not morally justified in doing so.

Here it is important to note that, at least according to traditional reasoning, we cannot show that a theory is either true or false by demonstrating that it has good or bad consequences. The fact (if you will excuse such a vulgar word) that Einstein's famous equation $e = mc^2$ led eventually to the horrors of Hiroshima and Nagasaki, does not disprove the theory of special relativity. If we are to disprove some forms of relativism, and with them the dramatic conclusions of Barnett and the like, we must find arguments which show them to be unsound. Fortunately, the efforts of many philosophers have, we believe, succeeded in doing this. The situation is much clearer concerning truth, knowledge and rationality than it is with morality and, most obviously, with aesthetics. Unfortunately, or you may feel that it is fortunate, the web of arguments can only be summarised here in a most superficial way. For a more satisfactory account we recommend some of the principal texts, such as Haack (1993; 1998); Norris (1997); Sokal and Bricmont (1997); Williams (2002); Baghramian (2004); Blackburn (2005); Lynch (2005); Sokal (2008).

Some forms of relativism, including the subjectivism mentioned earlier, are self-refuting. If there are no universal truths, then relativism cannot be universally true, since that is a non-relativist claim, and if there is no objective truth then subjectivism is just the subjectivist's opinion. Another common feature of relativist arguments is that they start by assuming what they set out to deny. Arguments to the conclusion that there is no objective truth generally start by claiming that there are different communities which have different truths, or that different scientific theories contain different truths and so on. But if these claims are not themselves objective truths the arguments cannot get started. Similarly, the argument that different conceptual schemes are incommensurable, so that one scheme cannot comprehend another, assumes that someone – presumably the philosopher propounding this form of relativism – is an exception to his or her own rule, and is capable of comprehending the schemes so as to see that they are incommensurable and beyond comprehension. Relativism about rationality and logic is incoherent and cannot even be expressed in any language, since such concepts as 'true', 'false', 'valid', and 'invalid', and logical laws, such as that forbidding contradictions, are necessary conditions for any language.

As we have seen, science is a principal target for postmodern relativists. They argue that, in trying to understand the world and ourselves, its stories should not be privileged above others. If truth and knowledge are relative, scientific knowledge is just one kind of knowledge among many and has no special status. One response to this is to point to the success of science and its associated technology. Our world and our life expectancy have been transformed by the discoveries of science and these developments are inexplicable if science does not, at least sometimes, give us objective truths and genuine knowledge. As Russell wrote (1959: 17), 'Science is at no moment quite right, but it is seldom quite wrong, and has, as a rule, a better chance of being right than the theories of the unscientific. It is, therefore, rational to accept it hypothetically.' Richard Dawkins (1995: 31–32) put the point more bluntly:

'Show me a cultural relativist at thirty thousand feet and I'll show you a hypocrite.'

Postmodernism and its associated relativism have never made much headway in the philosophy of science and we suggest that they are destined, like Freudian psychodynamic theory, to fade from the scientific arena and survive chiefly amongst novelists, playwrights and the devotees of cultural studies. Objective truth and genuine knowledge are credible notions, and they are things of value well worth pursuing. Relativism is most seductive where, it can be argued, things are a matter of opinion. No doubt postmodernism will continue to influence literary and art criticism, but these disciplines will continue to develop new methods of analysis and evaluation despite this. Moral relativism, of one form or another, has always been popular but there are strong alternatives including realist theories of morality (for example Dancy 1993; Smith 1994; 2004; Baghramian 2004).

Of course this discussion has been one-sided since we have not presented the arguments of the postmodernists and relativists in any detail, but we hope it has been sufficient to show that sweeping claims, such as those of Barnett (2000), are unjustified. Appeals to relativism do not show that universities must be radically transformed or that they cannot continue to fulfil the functions we list in 9.1. As we have argued, the real threats to our universities are economic and political.

9.5 The Choice

It is obvious that we believe that the first of the scenarios outlined in the Universities UK report (2008b) – the 'slow adaptation to change' – is the least objectionable. This is because it preserves a university system which stands a chance of fulfilling the functions listed in Section 9.1, while retaining some of the virtues of the present system. However, given our excoriating discussion of aspects of the existing university sector, it is clear that even the first scenario will not do as it stands.

The main problem is finance. Higher education may be a necessity in a modern society but there are many other necessities and all have to be paid for. Democratic governments find it easy to promise the benefits of a policy but difficult to extract the money to pay for it. As we argued in earlier chapters the result, as seen in Britain, is that there is an attempt to get the benefits without adequate funding, with very damaging effects. The consequences for individuals and society as a whole are serious: if we do not get higher education right, people are cheated of a proper education and society does not flourish as it should. In societies like Britain, which have long established class divisions, large differences in wealth and even larger differences in aspirations and expectations, the injurious effects are not evenly distributed. The wealthy and the privileged preserve for themselves the best, and engineer an inferior alternative for the rest. One result has been that a vast expansion of higher education has had little if any effect on social mobility or feelings of equality and fairness.

If our account is right and the effects of excessive parsimony and the taste for market models are seriously mistaken, we can see how much more damage will be done if the same policies continue. Indeed, Britain and similar nations teeter at the top of a very steep and slippery slope. If, in the dubious cause of saving taxpayers' money, we push the higher education sector in the direction of a more competitive, privatised, student financed and employer directed system, we will generate a tertiary sector irredeemably different from the one we have and with all the present defects magnified a thousandfold. Although the 'market-driven and competitive' and the 'employer-driven flexible learning' scenarios (Universities UK 2008b) are seductive and one or other is the most likely to be chosen by our politicians, we suggest that this will be a disaster.

In matters of finance, our recommendations are for two major changes. First, an increase in state funding of universities, including the amount paid per student. Second, a return to free higher education for all suitable candidates: that is a return to a system of student grants and the abolition of tuition fees. These changes would have to be accompanied by others. Universities must become more efficient. This would involve ensuring that income is directed towards the primary activities of education and research, rather than those who manage them. Management structures and the number of people involved in them would have to be made public and justified. There should be financial incentives for doing more with less bureaucracy. Some functions such as legal and wages departments could be shared. Universities should be encouraged to co-operate with each other in ways which reduce the cost of expensive teaching and research: sharing of resources, research facilities, information and so on. The RAE must be modified to encourage research teams to consist of the best people with the best ideas, rather than those who happen to work in a particular institution. The cost of student grants should be recouped by means of a properly progressive income tax: if university qualifications ensure a higher income then the beneficiaries could and should pay. There could be a system by which patents taken out by commercial concerns, which were ultimately dependent upon or derived from fundamental research, should pay into a research fund to benefit the institutions which carried out the research.

The size of the university sector should be decided by three factors: the number of people who are suited to higher education according to fair academic criteria; the number of that group who wish to attend university, and the nation's capacity to finance the sector. All three are highly manipulable. It was amazing how many working class youngsters suddenly transformed from dullards into potential university students when the opportunity was opened to them, and there may be equally amazing changes when the aspirations of state school students are raised to those attending public schools.

As to finance, that is overwhelmingly a matter of priorities, but investment in universities brings wealth and other riches back to society while, for example, tanks and aircraft carriers rust. The importance of targets, such as that of recruiting 50 per cent of young people by 2010, should be reduced: the aspiration may be a good thing but it is the cart not the horse.

One very contentious issue is the relationship between the higher education sector and, what in Britain is called, 'further education'. There is a clamour for more people with practical skills suited to be builders, carpenters, plumbers, electricians, practical engineers, draughtsmen, medical technicians, caterers, care staff and so on. Alongside this is the pressure for a return to in-job training and apprenticeships. In the past distinctions between polytechnics, colleges of higher education and universities were judged to be undesirable and those distinctions have been largely removed. Perhaps it is time to continue the process and allow some universities to combine with colleges of further education. This would enable those universities to have a closer association with industry but without prejudicing their university status or compromising their academic activities. There would then be distinctions between qualifications but not institutions.

The substance of the critique conducted in the earlier chapters reduces to the argument that *all* universities should offer a proper university education, delivered in a proper way and conducted in an appropriate atmosphere. What 'proper' and 'appropriate' mean here has been hinted at in this and earlier chapters, and will be elaborated in those that follow. The ideal is the prized 'liberal education'. While it is healthy that universities should specialise in different areas, it is important that they all aspire to serving the functions listed in 9.1, and that they all aim for the depth and breadth of learning that characterises a university education. It is equally important that they all try to foster that intellectual and scholarly ethos that is so characteristic of a good university, yet so difficult to describe. This may require some of them to modify or abandon their modular degrees, adjust their teaching procedures to alleviate the worst effects of mass education, and transform their management structures to give academics greater autonomy. These and other changes will be discussed in the following chapters.

In this chapter we have tried to outline what kind of thing we think a university should be. We began by stating boldly, but in broad terms, what functions we believe a university should serve. After a sketch of the principal factors which may act within a society to determine the size and nature of its higher educational system, we examined some of the possible routes the UK could take in moulding such a system, bringing out their merits and, chiefly, their dangers. After a wrestle with some more abstract or philosophical obstacles we have outlined, in broad terms, what we consider would be an ideal worth working towards. As the reader will have gathered from the earlier chapters and summarised here, we feel that the university sector, as it is today, falls short of that ideal and some parts of it have serious faults which need to be changed, despite having some institutions that are among the world's best. In the remaining chapters we will make some constructive suggestions to this end. They will mostly concern the practices of teaching and learning within the institutions. If the above recommendations about finance were followed the task of improving the system would be made much easier. If other routes are taken, as seems likely, our suggestions for reform will be less relevant or more difficult to achieve.

10
Coping with Change

It would be difficult to find an article or text about the current state of higher education which did not rehearse a litany of changes with which the system has been confronted, and the tone will very often be negative. We too have made several criticisms of the recent journey into mass education, and it does not seem unreasonable to claim that those involved in the "industry" are unhappy with where they have been led. With change comes trouble.

Some of the troubles are associated with changes in the nature of the work people do and the status that goes with it. For example, today the academics often feel beleaguered: transformed into a minority and witnessing their own inexorable absorption into a mass of staff. For those for whom this transformation has come as a surprise there is little sanctuary to be found in the lecture theatres, seminar rooms and labs. Instead of relatively passive students, fulfilling their side of the bargain with varying degrees of enthusiasm, there are now diverse groups of "customers" who demand that assignments are returned quickly and with favourable marks – after all, it's not their fault if they are awarded a low grade – who fiddle with MP3 players, make and take phone calls and text during classes, or record sessions 'For me mate'. No surprise then that some academics of a traditional bent shun, whenever possible, the uncertainties of the classroom, retreating to whatever haven appears to offer sanctuary.

Is this a pastiche – a grotesque and dystopian representation of reality, more at home in one of Tom Sharpe's novels or the University of Poppleton? To some this picture would be unjust and at odds with their own experience of teaching, but to a substantial number this Bruegelesque representation could pass for reality.

Changes are certainly happening. We now need market sensibilities where once we needed enthusiasm. What should we be teaching? How might we attract student customers to fill our programmes and how can we keep them? How can we steal a march on our competitors? The days when we simply designed and ran the programmes we judged to be of value are long gone, having been replaced by the need to spot a possible market and address it, until that particular opportunity is exhausted, by which time we need to have spotted another. Managing learning, whether it occurs within or without the conventional classroom, is rendered difficult and questionable. What does the private sector want? Does it even know? There is a need to expand the range of courses we offer and find ways of recruiting from previously neglected populations, but how? Ought we to offer e-learning? What technology will we need? What is the latest technology? And who should make these decisions and do the managing? To this we can add the problem of anticipating the demands from government, the impact of international agreements, predicting future funding and so on.

Here we will examine just a sample of the many changes, focusing on some of the new courses that have come along with widening participation; the bewildering revolutions in technology; the snarl of issues concerning management, and new pressures coming from outside the whole education sector.

10.1 Widening Participation

The recent decade has witnessed the introduction of vigorous policies designed to encourage more vocationally oriented programmes; many within further education, but increasingly within the higher education sector. This trend has tended to sharpen the debate concerning the purposes of the university: whether it is to serve the needs of the nation and its economic survival, or whether it is to provide a broad, liberal education which enables individuals to flourish. Of particular interest to the authors is the blossoming of foundation degrees and work-based learning schemes: both manifestations of the widening participation initiative.

Foundation degrees have shipped their fair share of adverse criticism, often being characterised as little better than glorified access programmes and of far lesser importance than the conventional undergraduate degree programme. Advertised as degree level qualifications designed in collaboration with employers, which combine academic study with workplace learning, they are intended to provide individuals with the knowledge and skills to improve performance and productivity; thus their utilitarian nature is explicitly acknowledged. Much is made of their immediacy of application, their flexibility in terms of modes of study and their potential to enable individuals to re-orientate their lives. It is not surprising then that many academics view foundation degrees with suspicion, perceiving in them the most recent and blatant expression of the policy-makers' desire to eradicate all vestiges of liberal education in favour of a soundly utilitarian ethic. To many, the foundation degree is beneath contempt. Others feel that this is to do the idea considerable disservice, diverting attention away from the potential benefits which might be secured. To pose the issue dualistically, as right/wrong, liberal/utilitarian, both distorts and over-simplifies the issue, whilst running the risk of perpetuating that training versus education divide which has contributed little of practical value to individuals, institutions, or the nation as a whole. We need to find ways of accommodating the change.

If it were possible to step nimbly between the rhetoric and balance the apparently competing demands for skills development intended to service the economy and that for developing self-motivated and autonomous individuals, then perhaps it might be possible to create provision which remains educationally sound. Possibly, foundation degrees could be designed with reference to such values as the overall development of an individual's potential and be managed considerately by means of pedagogic regimes which attempt to respond to the needs of the students. They might be assessed in ways which satisfy the employers' needs for skills, whilst supporting and consolidating learning and personal development. Perhaps then they would represent a powerful educational tool.

However, the foundation degree presents curriculum designers and teachers with some interesting challenges. Not the least of these being the establishment of robust and productive relationships with employers and those occupational groups which have responsibility for the setting and maintenance of standards within specific sectors. Whilst all parties may well have firm convictions in terms of what is required, the negotiations to engineer coherent programmes take time, patience and the coming together of cultures which appear to have little in common. Each constituency of interest has to engage in a process of learning and adaptation until they develop an understanding of each other's positions, but this is time well spent.

The experience of working with participants on foundation degrees is one which has much to recommend it. Whilst initial expectations tend to focus on the immediate – How can I use this? Where does this fit? – that focus can be used to broaden out the attention, interest and motivations of participants. The exploration of the immediate can be used to prompt questions and reflections on how this or that happens to be the case – Why is it this way? A shift can occur from the immediate and unconsidered resolution of issues and problems to the reasons behind beliefs and actions. In short, a sensitive pedagogy can foster the development of that process of critical reflection which involves, '. . . the bringing together of one's assumptions, premises, criteria and schemata into consciousness and vigorously critiquing them' (Mezirow 1985: 25).

Foundation degrees are popular with mature students and it has long been acknowledged that they bring with them an invaluable stock of knowledge and experience which can be drawn upon by the teacher to promote and support learning. But, they can also bring less useful baggage, especially fear of examinations, essay writing and other unfamiliar tasks. Assessment, long the principal determinant of students' attention, can loom threateningly before them. Unaccustomed to writing in a formal academic register or indeed unused to writing much at all, it is easy for doubts to convert themselves into fears which can paralyse. Aware of these dangers, universities include 'Writing for academic purposes' provision into their induction programmes, in which the strictures of academic discourse are set out. Their success is questionable, especially with students whose eyes are set on a practical training.

In order to demonstrate the ability to think and express oneself critically and analytically, is the academic register the only means of expression? Accepting that learning involves the acquisition of knowledge and capabilities in areas which formerly were unfamiliar to the individual, does the possession of the ability to write in an academic style represent the principal priority, or might there be other qualities and capabilities which the student should be expected to demonstrate? It may be that we need to become more imaginative.

The principal intentions of a university education are that it should promote the ability to think critically, consider evidence and be discriminating in its selection and use, but it is entirely possible that such capabilities can be expressed in forms other than the traditional essay or extended piece of narrative work. Forms could be employed which are more relevant and appropriate to the individual student and their workplace, such as the report, the presentation or pitch. Even policy statements and briefings can be used to demonstrate the ability to operate with knowledge, exercise discrimination, and judge relevance and appropriateness.

We have stressed before that students want and respond best to feedback that is prompt and helpful. Research confirms the rule of thumb that 'quick and dirty' feedback is better than late and detailed. Whilst we would not dispute that there is a role for detailed feedback, prompt, formative feedback is both the most useful and the most popular. There are a number of ways in which this can be achieved. Perhaps traditional classroom-based approaches, whether collective or on a one-to-one basis, can be more subtle and sensitive, but e-learning approaches such as blogs, podcasts or the common email, can specify assignment requirements and give almost immediate feedback on early drafts.

We have found in a range of foundation degree programmes that an adaptation of the Patchwork Text approach to assessment can provide formative feedback and flexibility, that can be progressively evolved into the more common summative format. The form of the Patchwork Text adopted was one in which each taught element had an attached Patch which participants could complete at a time convenient to themselves. The number of patches varied, but participants were usually required to complete and submit 50 per cent, along with a critically reflective summary outlining what they had learned, how they had applied that knowledge and what the outcomes of those applications were. There is an overall progression from the initial patches where the emphasis is on the development of descriptive and basic analytical skills, through the more intensive analysis of interventions and applications to more critical analyses in the final stages. Experience has demonstrated the benefits to participants of being able to submit early drafts of patches for comment and formative feedback, and also being able to choose which patches to complete and when to submit them. On a number of occasions, on programmes involving participants from the armed forces and the security and event management industries – individuals who are frequently required to travel and work abroad at short notice – there are particular advantages to being able to programme in their assignments to fit their schedules. An account of this approach in action may be found in Dalrymple and Smith (2008).

The work and problem-based nature of foundation degrees also raises some interesting issues concerned with the role of theory. In conventional programmes it is usual that theory is presented and elaborated prior to its application to particular cases, scenarios or problems; however in work-based programmes, whilst following an overall scheme of content broken down into topics, it is possible to reverse this process and use theory to explore, illuminate and gain insights into specific problems. This enables the teacher to introduce a topic and elicit from the group examples of it in operation in the work-based setting. Quite apart from the obvious advantages of starting from the students' experience, it encourages them to value their own and others' contributions and, facilitated by the teacher, to begin to identify similarities, differences and other incidences of that broader phenomenon which is the focus of the learning. Thus groups can be moved from the descriptive to the analytical and to an appreciation of the value of theories. Once fired by the possibilities and insights that relevant theory can generate, students perceive its value and will become positively voracious in both reading and discussion, in class and out of it. This situation is particularly gratifying to the teacher, representing Schein's (1988) claim that there is nothing so practical as a good theory.

It remains a question whether foundation degrees and other forms of work-based learning should be counted part of higher education and within the province of universities. The issue is partly one of the extent to which the work-based nature of the programme is considered central to it and how it fits with the broader educational intentions of the programme. Our experience suggests that it is possible for there to be significant theoretical and critical content in foundation degrees, and that they can achieve a worthy educational standard. Just as medical students spend time in placements, so can students with other vocations. However, medical degrees are long while foundation degrees are short, although they can often be extended to obtain an honours degree. Such nice distinctions and questions of rank might be rendered unnecessary if universities were able join with colleges of further education and offer a wide range of courses.

10.2 The Promise of Technology

If there is a single factor which illustrates the changes that have occurred in the higher education sector, and continue to do so, it is perhaps the introduction and proliferation of learning technology. In a dramatically short period of time we have moved from those great grey, square metal boxes operating on little more than candle power to laptops little larger than a paperback and iPhones through which we can check our schedules, send and receive emails, access websites, follow satnav and log our travelling expenses. Simultaneously, it would appear that time has accelerated, as we do more varied tasks in a fraction of the time it once required, only to find that there is another tranche of tasks hurtling towards us out in the ether. Opportunities to lean back in the chair, glance out of the window and mutely commend ourselves for having done not too bad a job of work have evaporated, filled with yet more demands and challenges. Opportunities, or threats? We barely have time to consider.

Technology has reached every corner of the professional lives of everyone within the university. Managers could not function without their computers; academics prepare their lectures on PowerPoint and can amass research data without even having to stroll to the library – which is, in any case, now a 'resource centre'. The speed of communication has enabled notes of meetings to be circulated within hours of the meeting finishing, or even before we leave the room. We can communicate with students remotely and, with the aid of cutting and pasting, reduce the time it took formerly to produce learning materials, reports and articles. Today's students, by and large, are pretty much wired in to the possibilities of the electronic universe, whilst the majority of those who teach them may lag some way behind.

From somewhat ad hoc origins, the development of learning technologies owes much to the work of the Joint Information Service Committee (JISC), which has in recent years been central to the dissemination of research, good practice and general discussion. JISC's research findings have been instrumental in identifying and plotting emerging trends which are likely to impact significantly on education in the future. The majority of students use laptops, mobile phones and social software in their daily lives, both for study and recreation; they seek choice and are used to flexibility and a degree of control over what they do and how they do it. Universities need to develop an understanding of this generation of students in order better to address their needs.

It is argued that we need to develop the skills of 'transliteracy', defined broadly as 'The ability to write and write using multiple media, including traditional print media, electronic devices and online tools' (Word Spy 2008). The concept of transliteracy provides a significant means of thinking about how, as teachers and others, we might make use of what is available to the best advantage of those we are responsible for teaching. Just as the concept of literacy implies the ability to adjust to and secure the maximum from a range of textual and graphic sources, so transliteracy suggests that, both learners and teachers need to be aware of the electronic opportunities which are available. It is a commonplace of contemporary technological developments that one has only to turn one's back, for whole sections of the technological landscape to have been transformed.

Amidst all this change, and in a situation where we cannot readily develop operational competence in all that is available, it is important that we ensure that we are aware of what might be possible, always accepting that further changes will render what we know provisional. In short, we need to develop those reflective and metacognitive skills which enable us to make the most appropriate decisions regarding what we use to support our teaching. Inevitably this will mean that different knowledge areas and individuals within them will arrive at different solutions and approaches to what might be termed the appropriate blend. Integrating face-to-face and electronic interactions, as Melville (2008) suggests, is at the heart of what will constitute effective learning and teaching. Students brought up on Google and Wikipedia will expect to be involved in their own learning but they must learn discrimination in the selection of sources and materials, and honesty in its use. Melville's report goes on to suggest that there will be significant changes in the nature of the relations between learners and teachers, as the former draw increasingly on their peers to explore and consolidate learning; interacting via social networking platforms such as YouTube and Facebook, and establishing discussion forums into which teachers might, or might not be invited.

Alongside this democratising shift in relation to information and knowledge, the desire of students to work more collaboratively will place increasing demands on conventional assessment systems, requiring them to acknowledge and accommodate collaborative work and peer assessment as well as the more traditional formative assessment and feedback. Melville suggests that this process cannot be held back, it is already happening and requires academic staff to begin to ask different sorts of questions and formulate more appropriate forms of assessment. Indeed, the recurrent theme in today's discourse is the dangers of the gap between students and tutors, but if it is possible for academic staff to become transliterate then, suggests Melville, both students and tutors can look forward to enjoying extraordinary and mutual opportunities in relation to learning.

Time, however, is short, but the thousand flowers of innovation can be seen in the landscape and it is essential that they are encouraged to bloom, for without the agency of the learning technologies, claims Laurillard (2008), the traditional teaching approaches and technologies cannot cope with the numbers of students. Technology has to be part of an overall strategy.

> Technology is never the whole solution. The recent history of technology in education tells us that however good it is, it achieves little without the complementary human and organisational changes needed, and these are always difficult.
>
> (Laurillard 2008: 320)

Evidence of innovations being effectively earthed into the lives of students can be demonstrated in projects such as that currently in place at the University of Hertfordshire, in which students are paid to mentor their tutors in software applications with which the latter are unfamiliar. Imagine that – students mentoring teachers! Though perhaps that is no more than the realisation of the old maxim that to teach is to learn whichever way the instruction flows. And Second Life, not so universally popular with students, but enthusiastically colonised by some universities, has provided art and design students with opportunities to reach vast audiences in order to assess the appeal of their work. Sounds Good, a JISC Project based at the University of Leeds, is an example of a small-scale innovation that provides digital audio sound files which can be accessed via their MP3 players by students. It provides them with feedback, both formative and summative. The apparently 'live' nature of the feedback has proved popular and the project is destined to enter a second and more extended phase.

What is abundantly clear however is that universities need, in Freedman's terms, to move from being 'intermittent electronic cultures' to realising the more integrated approach of an electronic infrastructure (cited in Higginbottom 2009). The thrust of the current cultural change is being recognised as primary schools are being urged to Twitter, to blog and to get involved with that community of practice represented by the likes of Open Source Software.

10.3 Changing Management

There was a time when academics did academic stuff and non-academics ran around behind them and made sure that everything worked, even to the extent of phoning academics at home to remind them that they were due to lecture. Most institutions have their apocryphal stories of confused, distant and distrait academics whose wives allegedly dressed them, drove them and generally ensured that they did not have to trouble themselves with the mundane considerations of life – the desk strewn with papers, the jacket over the chair and the bacillus emerging from the coffee cup are still, just, the stuff of memory. It is no longer so clear that we can simply label people as academics and non-academics, the latter being a slightly derogatory term. Today those 'docile clerks', the secretaries, registrars, technicians, lab assistants, student counsellors, advisers and managers, are less easily corralled into a pen outside the senior common room. This is not just because some, the managers especially, have gained more powers than the academics. It is also because many of their roles mean that they are engaged with students and the teaching process just as much as the teaching staff. We have to cope with these changes and change management to do so.

Celia Whitchurch's (2006) Interim Report entitled 'Professional Managers in UK Higher Education: Preparing for Complex Futures' eloquently charts the emergence of the professional manager whose remits take them into areas previously managed, or not managed, by academics. She says that these 'blended professionals' are increasingly occupying those ambiguous and 'quasi-academic territories . . . in which professional managers' activities converge and overlap with those of academics and other colleagues' (Whitchurch 2006: 5). They cross functional boundaries, often performing translational and interpretative functions between the different constituencies both within and without the university.

Whitchurch charts the transformation from a community of scholars into a 'community of professionals', tracing that range of terms which have been used to describe the work of these hybrid, multi-professionals as they have begun to realise for themselves distinct identities and assume responsibility for functions ranging from human resources and marketing to skills support, information and IT services. The lines between the academic and this range of additional roles and functions are blurring, boundaries are being rendered permeable or non-existent. Yet, at the same time, clear fracture lines are appearing between staff groupings, particularly between the academic staff and the increasing numbers of professional managers. Lines have been drawn, positions assumed and polarities established within a context in which, as Whitchurch (2006: 9) quoting Dearlove (1998) notes, 'academics want to govern themselves, but they rarely want to manage; they are often poor managers when they do manage; and yet they deny the rights of management to others'.

There is evidence that professional managers experience conflicting identities; if they adopt a service role then they become docile clerks, however if they affirm themselves and contribute to decision and policy-making they are accused by academic staff of becoming overly powerful. The all too ready resort to dualities bedevils and confuses the situation further as Whitchurch points out by reference to the work of Gornitzka and Larsen (2004: 456):

> The discussion on administrative issues is often made unnecessarily simplistic and confusing, either on account of the lack of a more fine-tuned vocabulary or the political character of the terms. . . . There is especially a need to overcome the prevailing simple dichotomy of administrative versus academic staff.
>
> (Whitchurch 2006: 10)

There can be little doubt now that the topography of higher education is changing as institutions seek to position themselves to maximum advantage in a hostile environment. Structures, roles and relationships which existed formerly, are no longer relevant in this changed context, boundaries disappear and the ivory tower is eroded beyond utility. Staff of all kinds are required to manage and move from single specialist roles to ones which require them to work on initiatives, bids and projects of variable duration, reacting to tight deadlines and venturing into settings for which their original education would not have prepared them. It follows then that as a function of these changes, more flexible job portfolios will emerge.

The notion of knowledge management, suggests Whitchurch, might help in exploring the diversification of professional roles. She cites Middlehurst who as early as 2000 and again in 2004 identified posts appearing which required their holders to cross boundaries between management and academic activities. These roles are difficult to place within prescribed boundaries and are referred to by Whitchurch as 'multi-professional, hybrids' whose responsibilities take them across functional domains as they undertake quasi-academic roles, such as delivering induction programmes, study skills and support, and in doing so reflect a need to engage with a range of communities of practice.

Whether we like it or not, the context is irrevocably changed but, as we argued earlier, the result is thoroughly unsatisfactory as it stands. We have a stark choice: whether to adopt a Svejk-like approach and assume a position of strategic compliance – "Humbly report, sir; I am an imbecile" – or to find a better, more constructive response. Since, especially in Chapter 3, we have aimed large amounts of opprobrium at unsympathetic and more simplistic forms of managerialism, we need to make ourselves clear. 'Hard' managerialism, that is, managerialism which takes little or no cognisance of the specific contexts within which it is operating, but seeks the achievement of its own goals by coercive means, is entirely unsuited to the management of universities, particularly with regard to the management of learning. However that should not be taken to imply that all attempts to manage should be rejected. Softer forms of management are required, which engage in consultation with the wider community of professionals in an atmosphere of mutual respect. (For a fascinating analysis and discussion of these issues, see Meek in Amaral, Meek and Larsen 2003.)

Perhaps a look at events further afield might be useful. Lessons might be learned from looking at a system of higher education not so different from our own. Given the ties and migrations which have taken place between the two systems, events in Australia might offer guidance, since their higher education made the transformation from an élite to mass system a little in advance of our own. One change of interest was the decision by the Australian government to bring together, seemingly overnight, two very different sectors of tertiary education: the Colleges of Advanced Education (CAEs) and the universities.

The two sectors had served quite different functions and had radically different management structures. The CAEs had provided largely vocational and craft courses of an applied kind, and they had very business-like, top-down managerial structures. By contrast, the universities, like their British cousins, were firmly oriented towards academic subjects and their organisation was more liberal, giving the academics considerable autonomy. This contrast may be familiar.

A debate developed about the virtues and vices of these rival systems. The liberal culture was perceived by many to have evident shortcomings, not least in its voracious appetite for resources, whilst remaining largely unaccountable. It was accused of introversion and the pursuit of eccentric and idiosyncratic goals. Supporters of the university sector argued in favour of the institutional autonomy and collegiality, seeing them as necessary for the maintenance of academic standards. The harder model of the CAEs, with its emphasis on professional management and rigorous audit, was seen by its advocates as more accountable and efficient. They argued that the close regulation and clear direction which worked so well in commercial corporations would benefit the education sector. Opponents argued that it was unsuited to the management of higher education. The mechanics of monitoring would become the end, rather than the means, of accountability, and personnel would:

> learn to respond to impossible criteria for their own and the institution's
> 'performance' by producing what are, in effect, command performances
> of *virtual* rather than substantial quality achievements.
> (Zipin and Brennan 2003: 362. Italics in the original)

In Australia, as in the UK, from the 1980s onwards the political climate changed in a neo-conservative direction. Free markets, ruthless competition and a thoroughly commercial perspective predominated. In higher education the romantic liberal, autonomous and self-regulatory regime made an easy target, since it relied for much of the proof of its effectiveness on evidence which was 'soft' and qualitative, whereas the corporatists could provide 'hard' quantitative evidence of success or failure – they could create league tables. A decision was made to bring the universities and the Colleges of Advanced Education together into one system, and pressure was placed on the former to manage themselves more like the latter. The result has been resentment, resistance and discontent on all sides. This uneasy ebb and flow between opposing ideologies has continued, to no one's satisfaction. The solution would appear to reside in establishing a balance between the two in which the virtues of each are acknowledged and accommodated. But how can this be done?

We could start by asking what, in the current situation, constitutes the 'professional community'. We suggest that the community comprises not only academics, but also that range of professionals whose roles contribute to the support and development of student learning at all levels, and to the maintenance of research. In short, we conceive of the contemporary university as a community of practice whose members are characterised by a condition of 'distributed collegiality'.

Distributed collegiality involves a willingness to contribute to, and share with, other members of that community, presenting one's ideas and offering them to the critical scrutiny of peers. It also involves accepting as peers those whose professional roles contribute to the central activity of the institution, drawing on their expertise and experience, and respecting them. It requires the erosion of existing silos, be they physical or mental, and participation in a democratic system in which each undertakes his or her role without interfering unnecessarily with the role of others. One further point is both obvious and yet crucial: the goal of distributed collegial management must be to facilitate the primary activities of the university – learning and research – and to serve the functions for which universities exist. This utopia will not be easy to build, but the alternatives seem so deplorable as to make it worth trying.

10.4 Some International Factors

Many changes in the UK higher education sector have been induced by our own government, but there are some that come from further afield: they are the result of international agreements. Now that we are a part of the European Community, various treatises and agreements apply to us and we have to accommodate them or offer resistance. They are opportunities for progressive change or challenges to good sense.

There has been interaction between European universities since their inception; generally friendly but sometimes not. Most have involved the movement of ideas, scholars and students from one institution to another, and many of the early universities were formed by the migration of groups of teachers and students from an existing school. For example, the University of Oxford may have had its origins – or perhaps a major boost in its numbers – by an influx of students expelled from Paris around 1167 or 1168. Naturally, theological and other ideas, theories, disputes and debates passed between universities, but so too did ideas about the proper organisation of the institutions. For example, the practice of organising groups of students and teachers into colleges arrived in Oxford from Paris in the late thirteenth century (Jones 2005). Learning, scholarship and research have thrived on this cross-pollination ever since.

In more recent times there have been various schemes for promoting the exchange of students. Perhaps the first was initiated by the Rhodes Trust in 1904. This was done with the now rather dubious purpose of strengthening and extending the British Empire, including the return of North America to its proper status as a colony, but the Rhodes Scholarships have since helped several thousands of overseas students attend Oxford University (Kenny 2001). Others, such as the Commonwealth Fund Fellowships – later renamed the Harkness Fellowships – helped UK students study in the USA. Alongside such schemes individual universities have organised innumerable exchanges of staff and students.

With the coming of the European Community we have seen vigorous efforts to encourage co-operation and exchanges between universities. The Erasmus programme, begun in 1987, has been the most important and elaborate of these. It has attempted to involve all higher education institutions in the Member States of the European Union, plus others with economic associations, including Turkey, Iceland, Norway and Liechtenstein. Well over a million students have availed themselves of this programme so as to study abroad, but the scheme is more than a system of exchange: it encourages co-operation in curriculum development, links between teaching departments, the use of a European-wide system of credit transfer, and so on.

If students are to be able to move from country to country for study or employment, they must be able to do so with the knowledge that their qualifications will be judged fairly and their applications dealt with by proper procedures. To try to ensure this, the Council of Europe and the European Region of UNESCO, together with several non-member states, signed the Lisbon Recognition Convention in 1997. This stipulated that the various degrees and other qualifications, and lengths of study, found within the signatory states must be treated fairly when considering applications. Any discrimination between applicants must be justified.

Few would quarrel with these schemes which have benefited so many students and academics, but there is not the same unanimity of approval for subsequent developments. European politicians soon formulated ideas for a more ambitious scheme. In 1996 the education ministers of France, Germany, Italy and the UK signed the Sorbonne Declaration which committed them to harmonising the higher education systems in their countries. This was brought to its obvious conclusion in 1999 when the education ministers from 29 European countries signed the Bologna Declaration. The chief element of this was to create a European Education Area, open to all European Union members and signatories to the European Cultural Convention of the Council of Europe. This involved the commitment to tidy up the clutter of different qualifications and periods of study that centuries of historical meanderings had left all over Europe.

At Bologna and at subsequent meetings it was decided that all nations should converge on a "three cycle system". A bachelor's degree would be awarded, typically after three years of study; a master's degree after a further two years, and a doctoral degree after a further three. Alongside this, there was to be a European Credit Transfer System (ECTS) in which a bachelor's degree would be worth 180–240 ECTS, and a further 90–120 ECTS for a master's, of which at least 60 would have to be at the second cycle level. No credit range was given for the doctorate. To ensure comparability and fairness, attempts were made to stipulate the quality of the degree programmes. The academic year was specified as involving between 1500 and 1800 hours of study and allocated 60 ECTS.

This neat and tidy plan has proved to be more complicated than it looks.

First, some countries have to change their systems far more than others. The Bologna process aims for a system closest to that found in the USA and fairly close to that in Britain. The German, French and Scandinavian systems are very different. As mentioned in an earlier chapter, the time taken to study for a first degree varies enormously over the Continent, from three to seven years, and this is further complicated by the different entry standard of pupils. Different traditions have given rise to very different expectations from students, especially concerning the number of hours they are required to study – both supervised and private. To this we can add the great diversity of teaching methods, the differences between vocational and academic courses and a range of assessment regimes and several other factors, and the difficulties of harmonisation become obvious.

It is significant that the Bologna Declaration was an agreement between politicians, not between universities or academics. This fact invites the question whether the agreement was made for economic and political, rather than educational reasons. The main purpose may be to provide a better education system: one that ensures a high standard, fairness and transparency. It may be advantageous to have more uniformity amongst qualifications, so as to aid in the fair treatment of students when they transfer between universities or seek employment. It could also be a device for promoting a competitive market within much of the world's higher education system, or for producing graduates and research at a reduced cost. Which of these different purposes apply and whether they are all equally benign and consistent with each other, time will reveal. Similarly, whether the relative weakness of the democratic control of these developments, instigated as they were by ministers, together with the tenuous connection with the universities, will result in a happy, co-operative process, remains to be seen.

There has certainly been some resistance. In Greece, students have taken over their university in protest and in France there have been several strikes against the changes. The reaction in Britain to the Bologna process has been more sedate, but there are problems. Some are very minor: at least since the fourteenth century, Oxford and Cambridge universities have awarded students who have achieved a bachelor's degree, an MA with no further study or examination. The MA is awarded after a lapse of 21 terms (seven years) following matriculation and was originally simply a licence to teach. Trinity College, Dublin has a similar custom. Whether these hallowed traditions will survive is at least questionable. The universities involved also award conventional master's degrees which require study and assessment.

However, there are more serious and complex issues concerning the UK. For example, the practice of passing from a bachelor's degree straight to a doctorate is widespread here, partly because of the expense of doing a master's degree in between. Another complication is that, as we saw in Chapter 6, students in Britain do not enjoy the same number of teaching and private study hours that are common on the Continent (Sastry and Bekhradnia 2007). Here the average is 14 hours of tuition each week, plus 12 more of private study making 26 hours per week in all. This compares with figures in the thirties and forties in most other European countries. Similarly, British first degrees take far fewer years to complete than many on the Continent. It will be interesting to see how these inequalities are addressed, given the increasingly arid financial climate in which UK universities are living.

Graham Gibbs has made some shrewd observations on these matters (Gibbs 2007). He has pointed out that students throughout Europe study for fewer hours than are specified in course documents, while UK students study least of all. Indeed, about a third of our students study for 20 hours per week or less, which means that they are, in reality, part-time students registered as full-time – the universities being funded as if they are. Much of this situation is due to the amount of paid employment sought by UK students, and he cites the research by Hunt, Lincoln and Walker (2004) showing the deleterious effect of paid work on the study time and ultimate performance of students, and similar findings in the USA by Plant, Ericsson, Hill and Asberg (2004). There are also cultural differences between European countries concerning the work expected from students, and there are big differences between institutions within any one country and even bigger differences between subjects within any one institution.

But things are more complicated still. Gibbs (2007) cites research by Vos (1991) showing that there is not a simple relationship between the number of hours of teaching a student receives and the number of hours they spend in independent study, so course documents indicating teaching programmes are not a straightforward indication of the amount of actual studying the students do. Furthermore, there is no simple relationship between hours of study and the quality of student performance. Hard work and long hours are important for good results, but they too are not related to the amount of teaching, but to the level of expectation set by the teachers. Gibbs (2007) points out that the biggest factor in encouraging hard and extensive work from students is the method of assessment. Citing Gibbs and Dunbar-Goddet (2007), he argues that the highest performance is found when the regime consists of formative-only assessment with extensive feedback and oral feedback. Students work less hard when faced with mainly summative assessment and least of all if there is little assessment of any kind. The reader will not be surprised if we welcome these findings.

We suggest that these observations have implications for the Bologna Process of harmonisation. It is clear that a merely quantitative comparison between degree programmes will not be sufficient: first, because the actual hours of study shelter beneath the camouflage of the official paperwork, and second because merely counting hours gives no proper indication of the quality of what is going on. The quality of the teaching support, the nature of the assessment methods and how the students use their time, are all important. It also seems likely that it will be difficult to harmonise degrees without comparing student finances and the different pressures to undertake paid work. If these implications are taken seriously, harmonisation will not be achieved by politicians or managers without the co-operation of academics and educational researchers. We can only guess at the games and manoeuvres that will go on between these parties.

There are obvious benefits that may emerge from the Bologna Process: harmony is generally preferable to discord. It will be a good thing if the quality of education is made more evident and equal, if that is possible, and the harmonisation may prevent some excesses such as the development of very short, intensive degrees. However, we have known, at least since Darwin published *The Origin of Species* one-hundred and fifty years ago, that variety and variation are essential for change. We fear that some innovations, including those we recommend, might be ruled out simply because they don't fit into the pattern specified under the Bologna agreements. It would be unfortunate if, for reasons of administrative convenience, we squeeze all of the higher education in Europe, and even further afield, into a single mould, without being certain that it is the best mould available.

In this chapter, we have discussed several examples of the problems brought about by changes and pressures imposed upon the higher education sector, both by its own internal evolution and by external agencies; and we have suggested tentative solutions. No doubt many problems remain, but we will discuss what we consider the most important amongst them. We have argued that one of the main sources of trouble in the universities, especially the newer institutions, has been the great change in the student population. The net has been cast more widely and it has caught, not merely a greater variety of students, but a shoal of new needs, wants and aspirations. We must consider how to face these changes.

11
Processing or Progressing Students

Not chaos-like together crushed and bruised,
But, as the world, harmoniously confused:
Where order in variety we see,
And where, though all things differ, all agree.
Alexander Pope, *Windsor Forest*

As we have pointed out in earlier chapters, there is a difficulty – a source of trouble – that lies at the centre of the great expansion of higher education. It is the obvious fact that as the recruitment of students increased from less than 6 per cent of young people in the 1960s to over 40 per cent today, inevitably students were drawn from an ever more diverse population: that is from a much greater range of social, ethnic and educational backgrounds.

In the 1960s the vast majority of young people in university expected to be there and came from families and schools which prepared them for what was to come. Of course there were those who drank or partied their way through the three years at college, but the majority were the brightest and most highly motivated products of the middle class. They knew what they wanted and what was expected of them and, with a few lapses and hangovers, managed to achieve it. The prizes were glittering and the drop-out rate was low.

Today things are different. There is a far wider range of levels and kinds of ability, and a much bigger variety of motivations, attitudes and aspirations. Many of those who once would have been excluded from university are just as bright as the best of those among the earlier élite, but the spread of ability is much greater. Students are drawn from a secondary education system that has been transformed. The public schools are still important, but the grammar schools have been greatly reduced in number and replaced with comprehensives, academies, faith-based schools and so on. The great majority of these do not have the subtle links with Oxbridge that the public schools had and still have. Preparation for university has been replaced by cramming for A-levels, and the feeling that entry to university was something close to a birthright has been largely replaced by a utilitarian calculation that, given the right examination results, the best course of action is to go to university. There is, of course, excitement and hope, but also a dim awareness that the prizes for most graduates have a modest glow rather than a glitter. One consequence is a drop-out rate that is costly to the individuals and to the country.

Universities have had to respond to these changes but in different ways. Oxbridge and the Russell Group of institutions have, it seems fair to say, changed the least. Worried by accusations of élitism and exclusivity, some have tried to find ways of attracting state school candidates, but done little to change their basic structures and procedures. The rest have been more inventive: they have introduced induction programmes, modified first year structures and adopted various means of coping with mass education including modular degree systems. Also, there is now a far greater range of degree subjects on offer, including some of a "pick and mix" variety.

It cannot be claimed that these changes have been anything near successful, and we have already seen that some have had a seriously deleterious effect on sections of higher education. Some things have not changed. It is still assumed that students will take precisely three years to go from A-levels to a degree, and that they will do so in three neat steps, each exactly a year long. Any student not able to do this is in serious trouble: extensions and repeated years are possible but are rare and expensive. Student drop-out rates continue to be too high with a disquieting, even demoralising, effect on both students and teaching staff. What is more, there has been a growing dissatisfaction amongst students, academics and employers about the quality of those emerging with degrees – hidden to some extent by the epidemic of grade inflation.

We suggest that there may be a different approach to this problem which, while radical and difficult to introduce in the existing system, might nevertheless have compensating advantages (Hussey and Smith 2010). It is a student-centred approach which rests on the idea that if students differ then we may need to treat them differently. The point of education is to change people in certain ways which are deemed beneficial and if some change more slowly or take different routes to their goals than others, then why not accommodate these differences instead of trying to iron them out? Of course, good teachers have always tried to adapt their methods to suit individual students where possible, but with the growth of mass education this has become increasingly difficult. To offer credit accumulation over many years, together with distance learning and e-learning, may be the answer for some, but it will be difficult to give anything approaching a traditional liberal degree by these means. Given that the luxury of one-to-one tutorials is unlikely to be possible in most universities, what can we do?

The answer may lie in the nature of education itself. As we have said, education involves changing people. The changes are of many kinds and magnitudes. A student may be changed by mastering a new concept, learning a new word, developing a skill, or being immersed in a whole discipline of study. The changes may range from the trivial to a transformation of the person. In practice, some of the changes that students undergo are beneficial while others are harmful: they may become confident experts in their chosen subject, or demoralised candidates for disaster. The process of education involves identifying what changes are desirable and finding appropriate ways of guiding students through them. The path and the methods will vary according to the variety amongst the students as well as the subjects involved. In an ideal system the education will exactly match the needs of the individual; in practice it will have to be a compromise, but not a one-size-fits-all mould.

Perhaps the most realistic approach would be to try to identify the most important changes – we can call them 'transitions' – that a student needs to make, and use these to construct a system that is as individual as possible. Instead of a Procrustean structure of terms, semesters and years through which every student must march, taking assessments in step with the rest of his or her cohort, we need a structure which is flexible enough to allow progression to be determined by the transitions achieved rather than the date on a calendar. The terms or semesters can stay but, within reason, students would face summative assessment when they were ready – or as ready as they will ever be – rather than according to a fixed timetable.

11.1 Transitions

'Transition' is not a precise term. Transitions are large, significant and complex changes that occur in a student's life: a nested pattern of lesser changes. They may concern their learning, circumstances, self-concept, autonomy, maturity and so forth. They are changes that the student, parents, friends, prospective employers and educators judge to be of real significance. Some may be intended and brought about by design, others may emerge by happenstance; some will be evaluated as positive, others negative. Examples include such things as the transition from home to university; from dependent youngster to independent adult; from novice to knowledgeable, skilled practitioner or from engaged student to disaffected drop-out.

Those involved in education have the task of deciding which transitions are desirable and which are undesirable and, amongst the former, the priority and order in which they need to be made. Teachers and other staff have to decide how to go about helping students through the important transitions and how to detect and measure progress. All this is just another way of describing what education has always been about, but describing it in this way changes the emphasis from an institution-based system through which students are processed, to a student-centred system which, at least to some extent, attends to the needs of the individual and their capacity to progress.

We suggest that the quality of the educational experience and the quality of the education produced could both be increased if the structure of a student's passage through university was guided by the way they make, or fail to make, the desired transitions. Such a system would, we suggest, help to reduce the drop-out of students and return some of the pleasure and fulfilment to teaching in mass education. The idea is that the teaching and learning strategies, together with the formative assessment programme, would be used to monitor and guide students so as to enable them to achieve the desired transitions, even when the process did not coincide with the traditional academic calendar. Before elaborating on this we will say a little more about the transitions we have in mind.

The transition that is of most importance to both the student who seeks an education and the system that provides it, is obviously that from naïve novice to knowledgeable, skilled participant of a discipline. This is the major or overarching transition that, together, students and educators seek to achieve, and it is what the final summative assessment is intended to measure. Of course, it consists of many lesser transitions: those within the various topic areas and sets of skills that make up the whole. Whatever the course or module structure by which the whole degree is sub-divided, the teachers will have to devise a system of teaching, learning and assessment that guides the student through the various stages. Thus the significant transitions will be the mastery of those important topic areas, each constituting a unit, course or module, and which together make up the whole degree programme.

This is familiar enough. However, those who are experienced in teaching will know that a focus on "units" of knowledge or circumscribed assemblies of skills is not enough. First, coherent pieces of knowledge do not always fit neatly into a term or semester, and the most educationally sound way of dividing up knowledge is to do so according to the inherent nature of the material. A study of the Victorian novel may require a longer course than a study of the metaphysical poets; a course on the philosophy of language may need to be more extensive than one on the philosophy of Berkeley. What is important is to devise coherent units of study suited to the level and amount of material thought necessary.

Second, merely to assess what a student happens to be able to repeat or do at a given time does not tell us what lasting education they have acquired. This, as we argued earlier, is one of the weaknesses of some modular courses. Tutors have to assess not just the transitory "knowledge" possessed by the student but what kind of knowledge it is, the attitude of the student to that knowledge, the value they place upon it, the motivation to use it and the confidence they have in doing so. Thus the transitions in knowledge, understanding and skills are closely bound up with other transitions.

Students enter university with a variety of learning styles and attitudes towards knowledge and their chosen subjects. Most will have recently been in secondary education accumulating A-levels and this will have influenced the way they learn. Many will have developed habits of superficial learning. As we described in Chapter 5, surface learning involves acquiring "facts", without much attempt at connecting them into a coherent picture or appreciating their relationships to other ideas. It lacks proper understanding and critical evaluation, and so tends to be inert – held in isolated ghettos and used only to do the necessary assessment, then released from captivity. Hence students must be helped to make important transitions from surface learners to deep learners. The latter, you will recall, is learning in which the student gains understanding of general principles and the ability to interpret, evaluate and apply their knowledge. It involves the ability to generalise and transfer ideas and skills to other areas of study.

Surface learning has the merit of satisfying the desire to collect modules or credits, but it has little lasting value to the student and even less to prospective employers. It is depressing to any teacher who loves his or her subject. Deep learning is for life. It employs habits of mind that are valuable in almost any kind of employment. It transforms the learner and his or her usefulness. The difference between the two kinds of learning is eminently detectable and so the idea of encouraging a transition between them is quite plausible. The design of the courses, the way in which material is presented and, above all, the way in which students are assessed, can bring about a change in either direction. Perhaps not all students can be transformed but, as argued earlier, some regimes are likely to be more successful than others.

Many students will have arrived with a utilitarian attitude towards learning: seeing it is a means to getting something else only indirectly connected with it – a qualification or certificate. Academics need to design their material, their teaching and their assessment so as to change the attitudes of their students. Ideally, the students will come to value their studies because they find them absorbing and value their learning because they see it as intrinsically worthwhile. This transition from indifferent consumer to involved practitioner is of the utmost importance in higher education. It has to be taken in stages: gaining an interest in one topic, then another, then seeing the interconnections, eventually turns a novice into a biologist, linguist, historian, philosopher etc., someone who identifies with their subject. There is an obvious interaction between the attitude a student has towards learning and whether he or she adopts a surface or deep approach.

Another vital transition for a student in higher education is that from a passive learner who has to be directed and motivated by others, to someone who is an autonomous person, capable of independent study and self-motivated to do it. Making the transition from dependence to independence is not just a matter of gaining skills and knowledge, or even becoming fascinated by a subject. It involves gaining confidence in those skills and in one's own ability to apply them, and the motivation to do so. It is not enough for the student to become capable of autonomous action, they must come to value autonomy.

To be autonomous a student will need some degree of metacognition: an understanding of the method of studying and learning he or she employs, so that they can change if required and conduct themselves in the most effective way. Autonomy does not exclude seeking guidance but it does mean that the student can decide whether they need help and whether to follow advice. There are degrees of autonomy and it is part of the function of formative assessment that the teacher judges what autonomy a student has achieved, and helps the process along. Kreber (1998) has investigated the psychological factors of both students and teachers that may help or hinder the development of autonomy.

There are problems with autonomy. One is the difficulty of specifying exactly what it is. The long debate about this (see for example Dearden 1972; Doyle 1973; Holec 1981; and Benson and Voller 1997) will not be continued here and the above account is offered in the hope that it is sufficient. Another problem is that not all cultures and sub-cultures value autonomy or see it as a goal of education (Pennycook 1997). We can only say that it is an important part of the kind of liberal education espoused here. However, it is possible that autonomy is sometimes out of place or dangerous. Merely because a decision is made autonomously does not guarantee its value, wisdom or truth. In most disciplines there are procedures for arriving at and justifying judgements, and these need to be respected. For example, a scientific conclusion cannot be justified by the strength of a person's conviction, confidence or faith. Hence there are legitimate constraints on autonomy: it is not synonymous with capriciousness. A fully educated person understands these restrictions: they may challenge them but only with good reason. Yet another problem is that the transition to autonomy may occur earlier in some disciplines than in others, and what is a welcome sense of freedom at a later stage may be a frightening lack of support at an earlier one.

The transitions discussed so far – in the amount, style and independence of learning – are vital, but may not be the most obvious to the students themselves. They are the kind of change that can happen almost without the person being aware of what is going on. The transitions that are most obvious, even painful, to the student, are those involving social and cultural integration.

The first of these is the change from life before entering university to life within the institution. Whether we are concerned with a young person away from home for the first time or the mature person who has been used to paid employment or the domestic life of bringing up children, whatever the change, it is a major transition and has been the focus of much research (Tinto 1975, 1987; Yorke 2000; McInnis 2001; Pitkethley and Prosser 2001). Most universities are aware of this and employ various induction programmes, "buddying" systems, mentoring, introductory sessions and counselling to help. These have to focus on the needs of the various groups of student rather than the convenience of the college, and they need to be carefully assessed to see if they offer what is really needed.

However, the social and cultural changes demanded of students as they enter and then progress through college are subtle and complex. Meeting strangers, making and losing friends, and settling into a new way of life, is complicated enough to bewilder the most socially adept, but there is also the task of becoming part of the university itself. Not only the university as an institution, but each discipline has its own "sub-culture" and language, into which the student has to be initiated. The ultimate aim must be to ease the students through all these demands with their personal well-being preserved and to the point where they "own" their chosen discipline (Bakhtin 1981; Gibbs, Angelides and Michaelides 2004). Ideally they will no longer see themselves as, say, students of engineering, but as engineers.

Beaseley and Pearson (1999), looking at Australian universities, discuss the fact that first year students have many different needs and cultural backgrounds, yet have to be socialised into the culture of knowledge (hopefully) flourishing in the institution. They have to become "literate" and adapt to rules and mores that are not always made explicit to them. Each discipline has a different sub-culture within the whole and there may be traps and clashes awaiting the student because of the conflicting demands – demands that may change as they walk from one lecture to another. Such difficulties may be magnified by some modular degrees in which students are expected to study several, very different, subjects in parallel. Even related subjects may make conflicting demands, as anyone will know who has, for example, tried to devise a research methods course suitable for both sociologists and psychologists. It is a challenge to academic and administrative staff, immersed as they are in the ethos of the university to the point of being unconscious of its strangeness, to help students by making explicit what is expected of them. What is more, this kind of assistance may be required throughout the student's time at university, not just in the first few weeks.

For many students, especially the youngsters straight from school, all these great changes will contribute to another kind of transition: a transformation of their self-concept. Broadly, we take the self-concept to have two components: one descriptive and the other evaluative. The descriptive element is the set of beliefs a person has about their personality, abilities including intelligence, creativity, tastes, powers, appearance, gender, political and social opinions, and their social standing – whether they are liked or respected. The evaluative component consists of their self-esteem: what value they place on themselves and their attributes, together with the degree to which they believe that they will succeed in whatever they attempt – that is their self-efficacy.

The idea of a self-concept is made all the more complex by the fact that it can change both over time and from situation to situation. A person may have several self-concepts depending on the social "role" they are playing or the situation in which they find themselves. As Stryker (1997) has argued, a person's behaviour may change according to the way they believe themselves to be perceived by others and by the demands made upon them in different situations. In some they are an authority, in others a novice. A mature student may be a mother at home, a minion at work and a student at university. There may also be differences between the concept that someone has of themselves and the idea they have of how others see them, and yet again how they see their ideal self – how they would like to be.

A student's self-concept, understood in this way, seems likely to have an important impact upon their performance (Dweck 1999). As transitions are made in a student's learning, autonomy, attitudes towards their discipline and social integration, their description and evaluation of themselves will usually change – but with some exceptions (Robins and Pals 2002). A young student with excellent A-levels who has been in the top set at secondary school, may become demoralised by finding themselves among far brighter people at university (Jackson 2003), or a mature student who has been for several years in a mundane job may feel their self-esteem and self-efficacy growing merely because a tutor takes their ideas seriously. Failure, lack of support, indifference from staff, sour relationships, financial problems and so on may lead individuals into the sub-culture of the disillusioned and potential drop-outs. A regime that attends to the pathway of each individual and lets them know that their progress is important, stands some chance of reducing these losses, even amongst students who are not over-endowed with either ability or self-confidence.

11.2 Using Transitions

It may be a caricature, but one that is not far from the truth, to say that the present university system takes a richly varied and disparate range of students and makes them march in step through a rigid educational mechanism which takes little notice of their individual needs. Examinations are taken when examinations have to be taken: at the end of a module or at the end of a year; then all but the failures march on to the next set of cogs. Of course, the academics controlling the process, if they take their teaching seriously and care about the students, may be monitoring just the changes that we have been discussing. They may want to see the desirable styles and levels of learning emerge, and witness their students gaining in confidence and autonomy, but they are so constrained by the mechanisms that the most they can do is give high marks to those who have managed the transitions and lower marks to those who have changed the least. At the end of three years, those who have survived will be spilled out with a degree reflecting what they were able to achieve in the allotted time.

This system is convenient, in that it processes everyone through the same programme according to a predictable timetable. Finances, staffing, room allocation and so on, are all easily managed. The students know how long their degree will take and how much it will cost. Despite these managerial advantages, we feel that a different, student-centred system might have advantages, both for the students and those who teach them. The idea is that a student's progress could be measured in terms of the important transitions he or she has made and that the time and resources allocated to each student would depend on their individual needs. The individual treatment would have to be kept within limits but would, at least, allow each student to progress to some extent at their own pace and in their own manner. This would require a system where some students took up to an extra six months or a year to complete their degree. Education rather than the academic calendar would be the thing of central importance.

Much would hinge on the methods of assessment used. The pattern found in most modular degrees is that each assignment is part of summative assessment: that is, it determines whether they pass or fail that module and at what standard. We propose the much more extensive use of formative assessment: assignments and exercises that are used for two main purposes. One is to identify the stage reached by the individual; the other is to use that information to help them move on to the next stage. The assessment regime would be a shared activity. Some of the assignments would be evaluated by the tutor, some by others in the same cohort, others by the student him or herself.

The main measure would be the degree to which the student had made the relevant transitions. The tutor would assess the level of knowledge and understanding, the depth or superficiality of the knowledge, the degree of independent working and so on. Other transitions – those concerning attitudes, values and confidence – would be determined, to the degree that that is possible, by conversations with the student. Progress towards summative assessment would, to a certain extent, be a matter of negotiation. There would be a natural incentive to make progress as quickly as possible and in company with other students but, if the system was well established, there would be little stigma attached to taking more time on some courses and no great glory in taking less time on another. Eventually each student would face summative assessment, but this would now measure not what they happened to have achieved in a given time, but what they were capable of achieving when allowed to do so. It would be a better reflection of the student's real abilities, rather than a snapshot as they are herded past the winning post.

This proposal rests on the assumption that the major transitions can not only be properly identified, but that progress through them can also be measured. Teaching staff would have to use the formative assessment to assess the degree to which the student has moved from novice to expert and from superficial learner to deep learner; from passive to active, autonomous student; from an attitude of indifference to the subject matter to someone who engages with their discipline and identifies themselves as amongst its devotees. All this demands skilled judgement by teachers. If talk of learning outcomes is appropriate at all, it is obvious that they are not the kind of thing that can be expressed in a list of bullet points. This may seem a formidable task for academics, but it is in fact what they already do, or ought to do, in their teaching. Indeed, it is what makes teaching a pleasure rather than a chore. The practical difficulties and inconveniences would be less significant once both the process of teaching and its products were improved.

Courses would have to be designed from their inception in such a way as to encourage the transitions considered desirable. If deep learning was desired then the content of the course, its length, the teaching methods employed, the teaching style and the manner in which seminars are conducted would have to make this expectation clear (Gibbs 1992; Rust 2002). Similarly, both the formative and summative assessment would have to measure not just what is known but in what way it is known: what principles are involved; what connections can be made with other material; what importance the ideas may have, and so on. The approach suggested here would also demand appropriate attitudes and motivation amongst academics. It would not suit those teachers convinced that attitudes, intelligence and other abilities are fixed, or who were indifferent to the enthusiasm they were generating amongst their students (Yorke and Knight 2004). It might be claimed, by those who are fixated on precise learning outcomes, that such things as changes in attitude and feelings of enjoyment are too nebulous and subjective to be measured by teachers. However, we suggest that those who have spent some time teaching find such things are detectable with far more certainty than is the acquisition of lasting knowledge. It is far easier to "mug-up" an examination answer than it is to feign enthusiasm and excitement.

Educational programmes designed in this way would require more than just a flexible timetable and examination calendar. Libraries, resource centres and research facilities would need to be designed to assist the transition from dependent to autonomous learning. If students are to start finding material for themselves or are encouraged to follow up lines of enquiry that interest them, they will require the resources to do so: merely to have a stock of "set books" for a module would not be enough. Teachers, libraries and resource centres must also become adept at meeting the diverse demands of independent learners.

Facilitating students in making the valuable transitions would require flexibility. While the ideal of treating each student individually may be impossible, it does not seem an unreasonable aim to allow, say, a two- or perhaps three-speed calendar of assessment and additional access to teaching staff. It would require smaller groups and better student–staff ratios than exist in many of today's universities. It would also demand a high level of skill and commitment by teaching staff, but the teaching would be more rewarding to both the teachers and the taught. The cost might be recouped by a lower rate of attrition amongst the students and perhaps even the staff.

Such suggestions as those discussed in this chapter face numerous criticisms.

They will be deemed too expensive, too demanding on teaching time, too inconvenient for those designing timetables and assessment regimes. They will be unmanageable by the universities, befuddling to the funding authorities and unpopular with the students who will not be able to predict the time-line of their studies. They might even be forbidden by the strictures of the Bologna agreement.

Each of these objections would have to be faced if such schemes were implemented. In the present circumstances it is unlikely that students will extend their studies if that means extra tuition fees, and it is no more likely that universities will give additional expensive tuition merely because a student needs it. These objections can be removed only by changing the present circumstances. Student finance and payment to universities would have to be changed. Management and academics would have to adopt more flexible processes: the focus would have to turn from the institution to the students. All this might be worth it if the result was improved education for large numbers of students, a better teaching experience for both teachers and taught, and a lower wastage of students.

What is needed is a state of affairs in which experiments, such as the one suggested here, are possible. Perhaps devolution in the UK, with its different systems, will allow such experimentation. Only changes that are justified by evidence are worth keeping, and that cannot truthfully be claimed for the present arrangements. Similarly, before we accept constraints from our politicians, they too should be severely tested – and that includes those imposed by international agreements.

12
Some Conclusions

Let us start by stating the obvious. Education is of eminent value and profound importance to any liberal society. But how should we interpret that statement? With our contemporary commercial habits of mind, it was tempting to see it in terms of an investment that a nation makes so as to get a profitable return. Like buying shares or bonds, we invest in education so that it produces the people and ideas we need to repay the expense and make us even more prosperous. There is, in this picture, a simple feedback loop: society invests in education and education repays with interest. By this means we can keep the tills ringing even in the face of severe international competition.

This naïve thesis had to be elaborated when it was realised that we needed to produce huge numbers of educated people and that the subsequent cost was enormous. However, the solution was plain: since those benefiting most directly from education were no longer a small band eminently worthy of the privilege, but an ample proportion of the population, they should pay more directly for the benefit. After all, it is only fair that those who profit most from a commercial transaction should at least defray the costs. In higher education this materialised in the form of student grants being replaced by loans, a reduction in funding for each student and the imposition of tuition fees.

Of course, the transformation of the university system from the equivalent of a family business to a massive industry required more than just money. It needed business sense, financial know-how and management expertise. The ethos had to change from that of a cosy gentleman's club to one of accountability and audit. If people are paying good money, then the product must not only be good, but measurably so. Since those working in the industry were experts in education and not in running a business, they needed to be supervised by those with the requisite skills. This might be resisted in the older universities where academics had long established privileges of self-management and autonomy, but in the newer institutions a more rational and efficient system could be installed. Shiny new brooms would soon sweep out the dust, increase through-put and optimise production; helped by the bracing breeze of a competitive market.

In the early chapters of this book we tried to show how this slick scheme had gone awry. Successive policy decisions produced undesirable consequences, especially in those parts of the higher education sector that had grown most dramatically to absorb the bulk of the increase in students – the new universities, ex-polytechnics and colleges of higher education. Put crudely, the new commercial ethos had transformed for the worse the experience of being a student, the nature of the education they received, the work of those doing the teaching, the life and status of the universities and the value to those who employed their products.

We cited as evidence the increased drop-out of students; their burden of debt; the growth of extraneous work to supplement their income; the decline in the quality of their experience of university life; the distortion of their relationship to their teachers and to education itself; and the dwindling value of the qualifications they seek. In parallel with this the academics have seen their autonomy diminished and their work engulfed by drudgery: the desire to do an estimable, or even a respectable, job of teaching has become mired in the ooze of under-resourced mass education. The atmosphere of trust and professionalism has slithered into one of audit and accountability. With only a smidgen of exaggeration, we can say that, in many institutions, the education academics provide has been carved up and offered for sale as a commodity, and even the skills and expertise involved in the processes of teaching and learning have been standardised and bullied into an auditable process of production.

With a similar touch of exaggeration we can claim that many universities have taken on the ethos of a business, the primary purpose of which is to stay profitable. To do this they must attract students by whatever means, prevent them from failing and turn them out with a level of qualification comparable to the competitor institutions – and all at the minimum cost. League tables, dubious degrees, grade inflation and the casualisation of the workforce, all play their part in this story. Meanwhile, the need to protect the excellence of our élite universities has begun to force a separation within the system: a divide between traditional, research-based, multi-purpose institutions and those that specialise in mass teaching.

There are aspects of these developments that are admirable. Our finest universities still rank amongst the best in the world, especially for the brilliant research they undertake. Hence the UK retains a high reputation and remains able to attract students from around the world. However, our finest universities are those that have been least changed by the developments of the last half century: they have grown, but their teaching and research procedures, together with their systems of management, have undergone only minor alteration. This is partly because their clientele has changed the least: they still recruit from much the same sections of society. It has also been suggested that the overseas students have become essential sources of income that must be attracted even if they are not of the best quality, and even at the exclusion of UK candidates.

The development of greatest significance is that there has been a huge and laudable increase in the number of people able to go to university, drawn from much more diverse sections of society than before. Many of these have achieved good educations and great benefit from their experience. However, there are problems. First, the serious inequality of representation between the different socio-economic groups persists in the UK. Young people from poorer families are much less likely to apply for entry to any university, and when they do apply they are much less likely to get into the more prestigious institutions. Second, although the new, enlarged student population is more diverse than before, with a greater range of ability, confidence, aspirations, motivation, personal circumstances and financial means, they are still being processed through a system, the essentials of which remain largely unchanged, and which does little to acknowledge the new range of needs. There have been some innovations to cope with the transformed situation and some, such as elaborate induction programmes, have had a measure of success. Other changes, such as the widespread introduction of modular degrees, have been much more questionable, and we have offered several arguments to show that this was a regrettable fashion which needs to be abandoned or greatly modified.

What is to be done? Where to begin? A starting point is at the heart of higher education: the processes of learning and teaching. We have argued that those who are engaged in these activities need to reclaim possession of them. To do this we must ask what our aims are, or should be. The learning community does not exist so as to distribute paper qualifications at the minimum cost; it is there to give individuals an education – an education valuable to themselves and those around them. The activities of teaching and learning must be motivated by appropriate ideals, not driven by managerial desires to achieve economical outputs. The ideal is what is described as a 'liberal education', albeit one that may be entwined with knowledge and skills which are vocational. The means by which this aim is to be achieved include designing courses of study and teaching methods so as to encourage deep, as opposed to superficial, learning. Students may leave as engineers, sports centre managers, politicians and so forth, but they must want to identify with their subjects and have a healthy, critical attitude towards them. Love of learning, enthusiasm for research, skills of scholarship and a lively and questioning mind will serve the person, their employer and the wider community, far better than an assortment of vaguely remembered facts wrapped in a degree certificate.

To achieve anything approaching this kind of education we need to break away from mechanical, linear, teaching programmes that usher students through a hierarchy of stipulated learning outcomes. We must employ a much more subtle and flexible approach to learning which allows students to visit and revisit topics, theories and concepts, so as to gain critical understanding rather than gather transient memories. Such learning must be guided by ample formative assessment: tests and exercises from which the student can expect rapid feedback and the teacher can judge the progress of the student. The aim must be to achieve not only sound knowledge of a topic but also understanding of the larger picture – the interconnectedness of the whole subject area. It is this integration that will give most satisfaction to those involved and encourage the enthusiasm and joy in learning and teaching that are so essential.

We have argued that it is extremely difficult to achieve teaching and learning of this kind in modular degree programmes that fight almost every aspect of it. If students are expected to take several small, unconnected modules at the same time, and move quickly onto the next batch, and then the next, it is little wonder that many end up with a fragmented and fading patchwork of the subject. What is more, if every assessment they face decides whether they pass or fail, it is not surprising that students become obsessed with marks rather than learning, and see their task as that of shopping for modules rather than studying for an education. We recommend that the length and form of courses are dictated by the nature of the subject matter and the teaching that is appropriate to it, rather than the conveniences of mass education; and that there is flexibility in how and when students engage with a programme. Perfect uniformity is essential when manufacturing buttons, but not when educating people. Fortunately, many institutions that employed modular degrees are already moving towards fewer and longer, more integrated courses. What would be ideal, would be an evidence-based practice, such that innovations could be tried and scientifically evaluated, our own included.

These recommendations amount to a plea for one of the primary activities of universities – teaching – to be taken seriously: as seriously as good teachers have always wished it to be. It is not good enough to devalue teaching; whether by passing it over to untrained research students or to casualised part-time lecturers, who see only their own module and have little idea of what other courses are being taken. Along with research, teaching is the main reason universities exist, and is certainly the main reason why students attend. The recommendations also require a move to a more co-operative relationship between students and teachers. We have tried to show how degrading the status of a student to that of a customer, and that of an academic to that of a stall-holder, has undermined the educational process. We need a learning community united by a shared endeavour and a network of duties and obligations, voluntarily entered into; not a market crowd out for what they can get at the lowest price.

However, we have stressed, more times than enough, that the rich and varied character of the new student population demands more than good teaching. Today's intake needs a flexible university system that can accommodate the great range of abilities, motivations and difficulties that such a diverse community possesses. It seems to us that we cannot avoid designing a more student-centred system that goes at least a few paces towards attending to individual needs. We have suggested that teachers could use their diagnostic skills to measure the progress of students as they negotiate, or fail to negotiate, the major transitions between naïve freshman and educated graduate. These diagnoses, in conjunction with the opinions of the students, should determine the progress through the degree programme, and if this requires some extra time and additional study for some students, this must be accommodated.

Changes of these kinds can only be achieved if the managerial and social cultures of the universities are appropriate. The atmosphere and ethos have to be such as to foster the co-operation and mutual striving for excellence, essential to a healthy learning community. The focus of the institution must be on its primary or central functions, not on production figures and finances. Academics can be expected to take teaching seriously, but they must not be forced to do that to the exclusion of all else. Most of the best teachers will have taken up their vocation because they have a passion for their subject, and to extinguish all hope of doing research and original scholarship is to scuttle their morale and shackle them to a narrow career. They must also be made to feel that they have a real measure of control over their activities. This is not an appeal for a licence to act capriciously: course design, teaching methods and assessment techniques must be appropriate to the subject and open to the sanctions of those qualified to judge.

Managers must be allowed to manage, but their aims must be to further the primary functions of the university. We are with Plato at least to this extent: a society works best when people serve the functions for which they are best suited, and resist interfering with others while doing so (Plato 1961: 433). We part company with Plato when we recommend that this virtue is best nurtured within a democratic system. All those professionals, including academics, counsellors, technicians, student advisers, managers, executives and so on, should be embraced within a distributed or broad collegiate system; a system infused with respect for each group and individual. Top-down dictation from an ever growing, and ever prospering, directorate is unlikely to produce the kind of communal life and atmosphere worthy of a university.

Of course, each university does not exist in isolation; it is part of a community of universities which, in turn, is immersed in the wider society. The relationships here are problematic. An element of competition between universities – for students and prestige – is inevitable and healthy, but to set them against each other in unequal combat, goaded on by league tables and quality grades, is to invite trouble. Individuals and institutions do drastic things in a war of all against all. Co-operation and the sharing of expertise and facilities have many advantages, including financial efficiency. With today's electronic communications there seems little justification for duplicating every managerial department and every academic resource. Co-operation in research, pooling the best ideas and widening participation could bring better results and raise the morale of those presently closed off from research. This would require modification of the RAE system for allocating research funds.

It may still be necessary to assemble a body like the QAA, for times when a thorough inspection is needed if an institution is in trouble. However, we suggest that the system of external examiners could become the best mechanism for exchanging good practice and ensuring quality. This traditional form could be revivified, with better training, better rewards and more intensive employment. We suspect that these improvements would cost less than the present arrangement. It should involve sharing experience and ideas, together with a rigorous critique of curriculum, assessment, facilities and student satisfaction: with access to what is really going on rather than the story printed on the paperwork. External examiners could be given more powers to seek information and insist on improvements, perhaps with the QAA as a body of appeal and adjudication. If the connections between examiners and institutions were changed fairly systematically, then a consistency of standards would emerge.

What the wider community wants from its universities and what it needs are not necessarily identical, and the same applies to governments. We identified seven vital functions for universities: to enable individuals to flourish; further the interests of society; preserve and promote our freedoms; create new ideas, products and processes; act as a repository of knowledge, skills and cultural capital; disseminate knowledge, ideas and values, and act as a gatekeeper to the professions so as to help maintain their quality and probity. We argued that, if possible, all these functions should be shared by all institutions calling themselves universities: this would be the safest, best and most equitable situation both for universities and the country.

The question of who should go to university has become entangled with macho political posturing and government targets. Figures such as 40 per cent or 50 per cent are entirely artificial. Our guiding principle, that is both rational and morally justifiable, must be that we should enable all those people to go to university who have the ability to benefit from such an education and the desire to do so, so long as the cost to society does not lead to detriments to people's lives which out-weigh those benefits.

Of course there are complications. One arises in specifying just what should constitute the "university education" that people must be able to benefit from. We have argued that it should approximate as nearly as possible to what was traditionally called a 'liberal education', even when admixed with vocational or applied material. If there is a widespread desire and a social need for a much more vocational training, closely associated with workplace experience, then a similar principle applies: those who can benefit and want to, should be enabled to do so, within reason. It may be found practical to affiliate colleges of further education with universities, so that the whole institution can offer a spectrum of courses and clear routes of progression through them, but we must maintain the different kinds and qualities of the educations offered. The Australian experience should warn us of the dangers of setting up competing systems.

Another, even more serious, complication with the principle is that it would require some difficult calculations involving values and priorities, which would change with such things as the wealth of the nation. We will almost certainly be told that our recommendations – especially those concerned with student and university finances – are unrealistic. Experience of a succession of governments makes us think that this prediction may well be correct. The financial and economic crisis that grips the world as we write makes it even less likely that money will be found. Yet surely the lesson the crisis teaches us is that, ultimately, the greatest happiness and well-being of a society cannot be achieved by the free market and the pursuit of profit, but rests on the quality of life enjoyed by all, and that, we argue, is intimately connected with their education.

The task of balancing the expenditure of effort, status and money on the many competing causes – education, health, welfare, defence, the banking system and so on – goes to the core of our culture and our central values. In a democracy it is the people who should have the ultimate say, but notice the implication: the people are only exercising a truly autonomous choice if they have the requisite information and the intellectual and emotional skills to understand it. That is to say, they must be educated, aware and motivated. The value of education does not come to us indirectly via the money it makes, whether to individuals or the nation. The value resides within us and in our society: it shapes what we are and the world in which we live.

This brings us to the nub of the matter. Education at all levels, including higher education, ought *not* to be a secret garden. Our culture, indeed the world's cultures, are the heritage of us all: to nurture, criticise, evolve and pass on. Everyone has the right to enjoy the flowers to whatever degree they are able.

References

Amaral, A., Meek, V. and Larsen, I. (2003) *The Higher Education Managerial Revolution*. Kluwer: New York.

Ash, T. G. (2008) Can we have world-class universities as well as social justice in education? *Guardian*, 29th May, p. 31.

Atherton, J. S. (2006) Heterodoxy: Against Objectives (Online. Available HTTP: <http://www.doceo.co.uk/heterodoxy/objectives.htm>).

Axelrod, P. (2002) *Values in Conflict: The University, the Marketplace, and the Trials of Liberal Education*. McGill-Queen's University Press: Montréal.

Baghramian, M. (2004) *Relativism*. Routledge: Oxford.

Bakhtin, M. M. (1981) *The Dialogic Imagination*. University of Texas Press: Austin, TX.

Ball, S. J. (2008) *The Education Debate*. Policy Press: London.

Barnett, R. (1994) *The Limits of Competence: Knowledge, Higher Education and Society*. Open University Press: Buckingham.

Barnett, R. (2000) *Realizing the University in an Age of Supercomplexity*. The Society for Research into Higher Education and Open University Press: Buckingham.

Baty, P. (2006a) Bonus culture sweeps the sector. *The Times Higher Education Supplement*, No. 1,764, 13th October, p. 1.

Baty, P. (2006b) Litigation fears lets cheats off the hook. *The Times Higher Education Supplement*, No. 1,764, 13th October, p. 56.

Beasley, C. and Pearson, C. (1999) Facilitating the learning of transitional students: strategies for success for all students. *Higher Education Research and Development*. Vol. 18, No. 3, pp. 303–321.

Bennett, A. (1969) *Forty Years On*. Faber and Faber: London.

Benson, P. and Voller, P. (eds) (1997) *Autonomy and Independence in Language Learning*. Longmans: London.

Biggs, J. (1999) *Teaching for Quality Learning at University*. Society for Research into Higher Education and Open University Press: Buckingham.

Blackburn, S. (2005) *Truth: A Guide For the Perplexed*. Penguin: London.

Bloom, B. S., Engelhart, M. D., Furst, E. J., Hill, W. H. and Krathwohl, D. R. (1956) *Taxonomy of Educational Objectives. Handbooks 1 and 2*. Longmans: London.

Bone, J. and McNay, J. (eds) (2006) *Higher Education and the Human Good*. Tockington Press: Bristol.

Bourn, J. (2007) *Staying the Course: The Retention of Students in Higher Education*. Report of the Controller and Auditor General. The Stationery Office: London.

Brecher, B. (2002) Fast food is no substitute for an intellectual feast. *The Times Higher Education Supplement*, 7th June, p. 18.

Brennan, J., Duaso, A., Little, B., Callender, C. and Van Dyke, R. (2005) *Survey of Higher Education Students' Attitudes to Debt and Term-time Working and Their Impact on Attainment*. A report to Universities UK and HEFCE by the Centre for Higher Education Research and Information (CHERI) and London South Bank University. (Online. Available HTTP: <http://www.hefce.ac.uk/pubs/rdreports/2005/rd15_05/>).

Brown, R. (2007) The greater good is not served by market forces. *Guardian Education Supplement*, 11th December, p. 10.

Bruner, J. (1960) *The Process of Education*. Harvard University Press: London.

Carroll, L. (1965: 1871) Through the Looking-glass. In R. Lancelyn Green (ed). *The Works of Lewis Carroll*. Paul Hamlyn: London.

Cook, R., Butcher, I. and Raeside, R. (2006) Recounting the scores: an analysis of the QAA subject review grades 1995–2001. *Quality in Higher Education*. Vol. 12, No. 2, pp. 135–144.

Cunningham, V. (2000) Fine mess we're in. *The Times Higher Education Supplement*, 13th October, p. 16.

Curtis, P. (2006) Black students failing to get into top universities. *Guardian* (*Education Section*), 3rd January, p. 1.

Curtis, P. (2008) University dropout steady at 22%. *Guardian*, 20th February, p. 12.

Dalrymple, R. and Smith, P. (2008) The Patchwork text: enabling discursive writing and reflective practice on a foundation degree in work-based learning. *Innovations in Education & Teaching International.* Vol. 45, No. 1, pp. 47–54.

Dancy, J. (1993) *Moral Reasons.* Blackwell: Oxford.

Darlington, C. D. (1970) The evolution of Oxbridge. *Question.* Vol. 3, pp. 37–51.

Davies, P., Slack, K., Hughes, A., Mangan, J. and Vigurs, K. (2008) *Knowing Where to Study? Fees, Bursaries and Fair Access.* Staffordshire University Institute for Educational Policy Research and Institute for Access Studies. Research conducted for the Sutton Trust, February 2008.

Dawkins, R. (1995) *River out of Eden.* Weidenfeld & Nicolson: London.

Dearden, R. F. (1968) *The Philosophy of Primary Education.* Routledge: London.

Dearden, R. F. (1972) Autonomy in education. In R. F. Dearden, P. H. Hirst and R. S. Peters. *Education and Reason.* Routledge and Kegan Paul: London, pp. 58–75.

Dearden, R., Hirst, P. H. and Peters, R. S. (1972) *Education and the Development of Reason.* Routledge: London.

Dearing, R. (1997) *Higher education in the learning* society. The report of the National Committee of Inquiry into Higher Education. HMSO: Norwich.

Dearlove, J. (1998) The deadly dull issue of university 'administration'. Good governance, managerialism and organising academic work. *Higher Education Policy.* Vol. 11, No. 1, pp. 59–79.

Descartes, R. (1985 [1637]) *The Philosophical Writings of Descartes.* Trans. by J. Cottingham, R. Stoothoff and D. Murdoch. Cambridge University Press: Cambridge.

DfES (2003) *The future of higher education.* A white paper presented to parliament in January 2003 by Charles Clarke, Secretary of State for Education and Skills.

Docherty, T. (2008) *The English Question or Academic Freedoms.* Sussex Academic Press: Brighton.

Doyle, J. F. (ed.) (1973) *Educational Judgements.* Routledge and Kegan Paul: London.

Dweck, C. S. (1999) *Self-theories: Their Role in Motivation, Personality and Development.* Psychology Press: Philadelphia PA.

Edwards, M. (1998) Commodification and control in mass education: a double edged sword. In D. Jary and M. Parker. *The New Higher Education: Issues and Directions for the Post-Dearing University.* Staffordshire University Press: Stoke-on-Trent.

Eisner, E. (2000) Those who ignore the past . . . 12 'easy' lessons for the new millennium. *Journal of Curriculum Studies.* Vol. 32, No. 2, pp. 343–357.

Evans, M. (2004) *Killing Thinking: The Death of the University.* Continuum Books: London.

Forest, J. (1997) Teaching and ambiguity. *Teaching in Higher Education.* Vol. 2, No. 2, pp. 181–185.

Fox, D. (1983) Theories of teaching. *Studies in Higher Education.* Vol. 8, No. 2, pp. 151–163.

Fuller, T. (ed) (1989) *The Voice of Liberal Learning: Michael Oakshott on Education.* Yale University Press: New Haven.

Gagne, R. M. (1974) *Essentials of Learning for Instruction.* The Dryden Press, Holt, Rinehart and Winston: New York.

Garner, R. (2007) Are standards at UK universities threatened by overseas students? *Independent,* 6th July, p. 37.

Gibbs, G. (1992) *Improving the Quality of Student Learning.* Technical Educational Services: Bristol.

Gibbs, G. (2007) *HEPI report commentary. a commentary on B. Bekhradnia, C. Whitnall and T. Sastry (2006) The academic experience of students in English Universities.* Higher Education Policy Institute: Oxford.

Gibbs, G. and Dunbar-Goddet, H. (2007) The effects of programme-level assessment environments on student learning. Higher Education Academy: Oxford. (Online. Available HTTP: <http://www.heacademy.ac.uk/ourwork/research/ teaching/projects>).

Gibbs, G., Angelides, P. and Michaelides, P. (2004) Preliminary thoughts on a praxis of higher education teaching. *Teaching in Higher Education.* Vol. 9, No. 1, pp. 183–194.

Giddens, A. (1991) *The Consequences of Modernity.* Polity Press: Cambridge.

Goldacre, B. (2008) Bad science. Missing in action: the trials that did not make the news. *Guardian,* 20th September, p. 15.

Gornitzka, A. and Larsen, I. (2004) Towards professionalisation? Restructuring of the administrative workforce in universities. *Higher Education.* Vol. 47, pp. 455–471.

Guardian. (2006) Letters and emails. *Guardian,* 6th May.

Guardian. (2007) Letters and emails. *Guardian*, 10th July.

Haack, S. (1993) *Evidence and Inquiry: Towards Reconstruction in Epistemology*. Blackwell: Oxford.

Haack, S. (1998) *Manifesto of a Passionate Moderate*. University of Chicago Press: Chicago.

Halsey, A. H. (1992) *Decline of Donnish Dominion*. Clarendon: Oxford.

Harré, R. and Krausz, M. (1996) *Varieties of Relativism*. Blackwell: Oxford.

Hart, W. A. (1997) The quality mongers. *Journal of the Philosophy of Education*. Vol. 31, No. 2, pp. 295–308.

Hartley, J. (1983) Ideology and organisational behaviour. *International Studies of Management and Organisation*. Vol. 13, No. 3, pp. 7–34.

Hasek, J. (1974) *The Good Soldier Svejk and His Fortunes in the World War*. Penguin: London.

Hefce (2009) *Core Funding/Operations: Allocation of Funds*. Higher Education Funding Council for England. (Online. Available HTTP: <http://www.hefce.ac.uk/pubs/hefce/2009/09-08/>).

Higginbottom, K. (2009) Technology storms the ivory tower. *Guardian*, 31st March.

Hind, D. (2008) The monster we don't see. *New Scientist*. Vol. 197, No. 2639, 19th January, pp. 46–47.

Hirst, P. H. (1974) *Knowledge and the Curriculum*. Routledge: London.

Hirst, P. H. and Peters, R. S. (1970) *The Logic of Education*. Routledge: London.

Holec, H. (1981) *Autonomy and Foreign Language Learning*. Pergamon: Oxford.

Hunt, A., Lincoln, I. and Walker, A. (2004) Term-time employment and academic attainment: evidence from a large-scale survey of undergraduates at Northumbria University. *Journal of Further and Higher Education*. Vol. 28, No. 1, pp. 3–18.

Hussey, T. and Smith, P. (2002) The trouble with learning outcomes. *Active Learning in Higher Education*. Vol. 3, No. 3, pp. 220–233.

Hussey, T. and Smith, P. (2003) The uses of learning outcomes. *Teaching in Higher Education*. Vol. 8, No. 3, pp. 357–368.

Hussey, T. and Smith, P. (2008) Learning outcomes: a conceptual analysis. *Teaching in Higher Education*. Vol. 13, No. 1, pp. 107–115.

Hussey, T. and Smith, P. (2010) Transitions in higher education. *Innovations in Education and Teaching International*. Vol. 47.

Ing, M. (1978) Learning theories. In D. Lawton, P. Gordon, M. Ing, W. Gibby, R. Pring and T. Moore. *Theory and Practice of Curriculum Studies*. Routledge: London. Ch. 7, pp. 61–70.

Jackson, C. (2003) Transitions in higher education: gendered implications for academic self-concept. *Oxford Review of Education*. Vol. 29, No. 3, pp. 331–346.

Jameson, F. (1991) *Postmodernism or The Cultural Logic of Late Capitalism*. Verso: London.

Jary, D. and Parker, M. (eds) (1998) *The New Higher Education: Issues and Directions for the Post-Dearing University*. Staffordshire University Press: Stoke-on-Trent.

Jones, J. (2005) *Balliol College: A History*. Second Edition Revised. Oxford University Press: Oxford.

Kamal, R. (2007) Fossilised curriculum built on fossil fuels. *The Times Higher Education Supplement*, 16th February, p. 13.

Kealey, T. (2008) Trust and transparency are frowned upon while degree inflation soars. *Times Higher Education*, 16th October, pp. 26–27.

Kenny, A. (ed) (2001) *The History of the Rhodes Trust*. Oxford University Press: Oxford.

Knight, P. (2001) Complexity and curriculum: a process approach to curriculum-making. *Teaching in Higher Education*. Vol. 6, No. 2, pp. 369–382.

Kord, S. and Wilson, D. (2006) Drowning in bureaucracy. *Guardian*, 27th December. See also the correspondence on subsequent days.

Kreber, C. (1998) The relationship between self-directed learning, critical thinking and psychological type, and some implications for teaching in higher education. *Studies in Higher Education*. Vol. 23, No. 1, pp. 71–86.

Kroto, H. (2007) The wrecking of British science. *Guardian Education Supplement*, 22nd May, pp. 1–2.

Lampert, M. (1985) How do teachers manage to teach? *Harvard Educational Review*. Vol. 55, No. 2, pp. 178–194.

Langford, G. (1968) *Philosophy and Education: An Introduction*. Macmillan: London.

Laurillard, D. (2008) Open teaching: the key to sustainable and effective open education. In T. Iiyoshi and M. Kumar (eds). *Opening up Education*. The MIT Press: Cambridge, MA, pp. 319–335.

Lewis, C. and Tsuchida, I. (1998) A lesson is like a swiftly flowing river: how research lessons improve Japanese education. *American Encounter*. Winter, pp. 12–17 & 50–52.

Loughlin, M. (2002) . . . Whatever that means. *The Times Higher Education Supplement*, 22nd March, p. 20.

Lukes, S. (2006) Pathologies of markets and states. Miliband Lecture given at the LSE March 16th 2006. Reprinted in *Crime, Social Control and Human Rights: From Moral Panics to States of Denial: Essays in Honour of Stanley Cohen*. D. Downes, P. Rock, C. Chinkin and C. Gearty (eds). Willan Publishing: Cullompton. Ch. 13, pp. 157–173.

Lynch, M. P. (2005) *True to Life: Why Truth Matters*. MIT Press: Cambridge, MA.

Lyotard, J-F. (1984) *The Postmodern Condition: A Report on Knowledge*. Trans. by G. Bennington and B. Massumi; Foreword by F. Jameson. Manchester University Press: Manchester. (First published in French 1979.)

McAlpine, L., Weston, C., Beauchamp, C., Wiseman, C. and Beauchamp, J. (1999) Monitoring student cues: tracing student behaviour in order to improve instruction in higher education. *The Canadian Journal of Higher Education*. Vol. XXXIX, No. 2–3, pp. 113–144.

McInnis, C. (2001) Researching the first year experience: where to from here? *Higher Education Research and Development*. Vol. 20, No. 2, pp. 105–114.

Malcolm, J. and Zukas, M. (2001) Bridging pedagogic gaps: conceptual discontinuities in higher education. *Teaching in Higher Education*. Vol. 6, No. 1, pp. 33–42.

Mather, K., Worrall, L. and Seifert, R. (2009) The changing locus of workplace control in the English further education sector. *Employee Relations*. Vol. 31, Issue 2, pp. 139–157.

Meikle, J. and Lewis, P. (2007) University heads warn of £10,000-a-year tuition fees. *Guardian*, 18th January, pp. 1 and 6.

Melville, D. (2008) *Preliminary findings of the Committee of Inquiry into the Changing Learner Experience*. (Online. Available HTTP: <http://clex.org.uk/emergingfindings.php>).

Mezirow, J. (1985) A critical theory of adult learning and education. In S. Brookfield (ed). *Self-directed Learning: From Theory to Practice*. Jossey-Bass: San Francisco.

Milne, J. (2006) Female students turn to prostitution to pay fees. *The Sunday Times*. October 8th, p. 7.

Moon, J. (1999) *Guidance for Writing and Using Learning Outcomes*. University of Exeter: Exeter.

Newman, J. H. (1976) *The Idea of a University*. Ed. I. T. Ker. Oxford University Press: Oxford.

Norris, C. (1997) *Against Relativism: Philosophy of Science, Deconstruction and Critical Theory*. Blackwell: Oxford.

Palfreyman, D. (ed) (2008) *The Oxford Tutorial: Thanks You Taught Me How to Think*. 2nd edition. Blackwell: Oxford.

Parker, J. (2003) Reconceptualising the curriculum: from commodification to transformation. *Teaching in Higher Education*. Vol. 8, No. 4, pp. 529–543.

Pennycook, A. (1997) Cultural alternatives and autonomy. In P. Benson and P. Voller (eds). *Autonomy and Independence in Language Learning*. Longman: London, pp. 35–53.

Peters, R. S. (1966) *Ethics and Education*. Unwin: London.

Peters, R. S. (ed) (1967) *The Concept of Education*. Routledge: London.

Pitkethley, A. and Prosser, M. (2001) The first year experience project: a model for university-wide change. *Higher Education Research and Development*. Vol. 20, No. 2, pp. 185–198.

Plant, E. A., Ericsson, K. A., Hill, L. and Asberg, K. (2004) Why study time does not predict grade point average across college students: implications of deliberate practice for academic performance. *Contemporary Educational Psychology*. Vol. 30, pp. 96–116.

Plato (1961) *Republic* Bk. IV, in E. Hamilton and H. Cairns (eds). *Plato: The Collected Works*. Princeton University Press: Princeton, 419–448.

Power, M. (1997) *The Audit Society: Rituals of Verification*. Oxford University Press: Oxford.

Push (2008) *Debt Survey 2008*. (Online. Available HTTP: <http://www.push.co.uk>).

QAA (2007) *Outcomes from Institutional Audit: The Adoption and Use of Learning Outcomes*. The Quality Assurance Agency for Higher Education: Gloucester.

Radin, M. (1993) *Reinterpreting Property*. University of Chicago Press: Chicago.

Radin, M. (1996) *Contested Commodities*. Harvard University Press: Cambridge, MA.

Ramsden, B. (2005) *Patterns of Higher Education Institutions in the UK: Fifth Report*. Universities UK: London.

Robins, R. W. and Pals, J. L. (2002) Implicit self-theories in the academic domain: implications for goal orientation, attributions, affect and self-esteem change. *Self and Identity*. Vol. 1, No. 4, pp. 313–316.

Robinson, K. (2006) Do schools kill creativity? TED Conference, Monterey, California. (Online. Available HTTP: <http://www.ted.com/index.php/talks/ken_robinson_says_schools_kill_creativity.html>).

Rorty, R. (1991) *Objectivity, Relativism and Truth: Philosophical Papers, 1.* Cambridge University Press: Cambridge.

Russell, B. (1959) *My Philosophical Development.* George Allen & Unwin: London.

Rust, C. (2002) The impact of assessment on student learning. *Active Learning in Higher Education.* Vol. 3, No. 2, pp. 145–158.

Ryan, A. (1998) *Liberal Anxieties and Liberal Education.* Hill and Wang: New York.

Ryle, G. (1949) *The Concept of Mind.* Hutchinson: London.

Sanders, C. (2006) Fees rise 'won't improve' quality. *The Times Higher Education Supplement.* No. 1,766, October 27th, p. 7.

Sastry, T. and Bekhradnia, B. (2007) *The academic experience of students in English universities.* Higher Education Policy Institute: London. (Online. Available HTTP: <http://www.hepi.ac.uk/downloads/33TheacademicexperiencesofstudentsinEnglishuniversities2007.pdf>).

Schein, E. (1988) *Process Consultation.* Vol. 1. (Revised edn). Addison-Wesley: Reading, MA.

Shore, C. and Selwyn, T. (1998) The marketisation of higher education: management, discourse and the politics of performance. In D. Jary and M. Parker. *The New Higher Education: Issues and Directions for the post-Dearing University.* Staffordshire University Press: Stoke-on-Trent, pp. 153–171.

Smart, B. (1993) *Postmodernity.* Routledge: London.

Smith, A. (1991: 1776) *The Wealth of Nations.* Everyman's Library: London.

Smith, M. (1994) *The Moral Problem.* Blackwell: Oxford.

Smith, M. (2004) *Ethics and the A Priori.* Cambridge University Press: Cambridge.

Sokal, A. (2008) *Beyond the Hoax: Science, Philosophy and Culture.* Oxford University Press: Oxford.

Sokal, A. and Bricmont, J. (1997) *Intellectual Impostures.* Profile Books: London.

Strathern, M. (2000) The tyranny of transparency. *British Education Research Journal.* Vol. 26, pp. 309–321.

Stryker, S. (1997) 'In the beginning there is society': lessons from a sociological social psychology. In C. McGarty and S. A. Haslam (eds). *The Message of Social Psychology.* Blackwell: Oxford, pp. 315–327.

Sulston, J. and Ferry, G. (2002) *The Common Thread – A Story of Science, Politics, Ethics and the Human Genome.* Bantam Press: London.

Taylor, M. (2006) Ministers failing to halt tide of university science closures. *Guardian,* 4th May, p. 13.

Times Higher Education (2007) World Universities Ranking. (Online. Available HTTP: <http://www.topuniversities.com/worlduniversityranking/>).

Tinto, V. (1975) Drop out from higher education: a synthesis of research. *Research into Higher Education.* Vol. 45, pp. 89–125.

Tinto, V. (1987) *Leaving College: Rethinking the Causes and Cures of Student Attrition.* University of Chicago Press: Chicago.

TLRP (2005) *Enhancing Teaching-learning Environments in Undergraduate Courses.* TLRP & ESRC: London.

Tyler, R. (1949) *Basic Principles of Curriculum and Instruction.* University of Chicago Press: Chicago.

Tysome, T. (2006) Workloads 'go through the roof'. *The Times Higher Education Supplement.* No. 1,763, October 6th.

UCU (2006) *Further, Higher, Better.* Submission to the Government's second Comprehensive Spending Review by the University and College Union.

Universities UK (2008a) *The Future Size and Shape of the Higher Education System in the United Kingdom: Demographic Projections.* Universities UK: London.

Universities UK (2008b) *The Future Size and Shape of the Higher Education Sector in the United Kingdom: Threats and Opportunities.* Universities UK: London.

Vos, P. (1991) *Curriculum Control of Learning Processes in Higher Education.* 13th International Forum on Higher Education of the European Association for Institutional Research, Edinburgh.

Walsh, D. (2007) Polio cases jump in Pakistan as clerics declare vaccination an American plot. *Guardian,* 15th February, p. 15.

Wheen, F. (2004) *How Mumbo-Jumbo Conquered the World.* Harper Perennial: London.

Whitchurch, C. (2006) *Professional Managers in UK Higher Education: Preparing for Complex Futures.* The Leadership Foundation: London.

Wilkinson, R. and Pickett, K. (2009) *The Spirit Level: Why More Equal Societies Almost Always do Better.* Allen Lane: London.

Williams, B. (2002) *Truth and Truthfulness.* Princeton University Press: Princeton.

Winter, R. (1999) University of life plc: the industrialization of higher education? In J. Ahier and G. Esland (eds). *Education, Training and the Future of Work 1: Social. Political and Economic Contexts of Policy Development.* Routledge: London, pp. 186–198.

Word Spy (2008) http://www.wordspy.com/words/transliteracy.asp

Wright, N. (2001) Leadership, 'Bastard Leadership' and Managerialism. *Educational Management & Administration.* Vol. 29, No. 3, pp. 275–290.

Yorke, M. (2000) The quality of student experience: what can institutions learn from data relating to non-completion? *Quality in Higher Education.* Vol. 6, No. 1, pp. 61–75.

Yorke, M. and Knight, P. (2004) Self-theories: some implications for teaching and learning in higher education. *Studies in Higher Education.* Vol. 29, No. 1, pp. 25–37.

Zipin, L. and Brennan, M. (2003) The suppression of ethical dispositions through managerial accountability: a habitus crisis in Australian higher education. *International Journal of Leadership in Education.* October–December. Vol. 6, No. 4, pp. 351–370.

Index

eBooks